The Deeper Walk

SPIRITUAL TREASURES OLD AND NEW
FOR SEEKERS TODAY

COMPILED AND EDITED BY STEVE PORTER

The Deeper Walk

Copyright © 2024 Steve Porter

All rights reserved.

Deeper Life Press

TABLE OF CONTENTS

DEDICATION

To all who yearn to draw nearer to God, may the words within these pages serve as a lamp unto your feet and a light unto your path, guiding you ever deeper into the profound mysteries and immeasurable love of our Lord.

INTRODUCTION

Dear Friends,

It is my great joy to present to you this beautiful collection of spiritual writings of The Deeper Life. Within these pages, you will find a wellspring of insight and inspiration from some of the most cherished saints in Christian history.

As you read, you'll discover the heartfelt wisdom of dear ones like Wade Taylor, who guides us into the high calling of Christ's Bride. John Wright Follette's reflections will stir your imagination to yearn of deeper intimacy with the Lord. Hattie Hammond's fiery passion will ignite fresh hunger to pursue holiness without compromise. Madame Guyon gently leads us by the hand into the restful simplicity of heartfelt prayer. Walter Beuttler's infectious zeal for God's manifest presence will leave you longing for more of His glory. And Seeley Kinne's prophetic clarity illuminates the path of the overcoming church.

But this is far more than just a book – it is an invitation. An invitation to embark on a sacred journey into the very heart of God. To lay aside the clamor of lesser pursuits and give yourself unreservedly to the One your soul most deeply loves. To be undone by His beauty, consumed by His affection, and transformed in the light of His glorious face.

As you linger over these anointed words, I pray that the Holy Spirit will take the coals of divine revelation and set your heart ablaze with holy passion for Jesus. May you arise from these pages empowered to love extravagantly, serve wholeheartedly, and burn brightly as a living witness of the all-surpassing worth of knowing Christ.

So come, the table is set and the Master bids you to draw near. Feast upon the delights of His presence as you commune with Him in these hallowed pages. And may your life be forever marked by the pursuit of the deeper things of God.

Hungry for more of Him,

Steve Porter

www.deeperlifepress.com

www.findrefuge.tv

www.oasisbible.org

FAN INTO FLAMES THE GIFT OF GOD

A Tribute - Wade Taylor (1924-2012)

"For this reason, I am reminding you to fan into flames the gift of God that is within you through the laying on of my hands" (2 Timothy 1:6).

This verse captures Wade Taylor's burning passion to ignite fresh hunger and devotion for Jesus Christ in the hearts of others. His life mission was to fan the flames of intimacy with God, reminding those he influenced to stir their spiritual gifts into blazing fires. Wade carried a unique presence of the Lord for one purpose: to spark a generation to pursue the depths of Christ and in doing so, prepare them for the end times. His life example continues inspiring many to wholeheartedly give themselves as kindling to the refining and empowering work of the Holy Spirit.

Just as Wade was set ablaze by key mentors (Walter Beuttler, John Wright Follette) in his early years, he later ignited many lives with the impassioned message, "This wonderful relationship with the Living Word is available for you...come up higher into more!"

Wade Taylor was a beloved mentor and spiritual father to many, including myself. I first met him in 1990 as an eager student at Pinecrest Bible Training Center, the school he founded and led as President at for twenty-nine years. Though quite busy leading the school, he made time nearly every evening to pray with students like myself who were hungry for more of God.

When I think of my times with Wade, I recall his gentle demeanor, compassionate eyes, and intimate walk with the Lord. He carried a tangible presence of God that imparted a hunger in me for deeper things. After praying with Wade, I would go to my dorm room and get on my knees or lie on my face for hours, letting the heavy manifest glory of God transform me. His prayers sparked a fire in my spirit that still burns today.

This fire was first lit in Wade by his teacher Walter Beuttler at Eastern Bible Institute in 1956. Beuttler instilled in Wade the immense value of waiting on the Lord in stillness and cultivating an ability to hear His soft whisper. He learned what it meant to make room for the Lord to come with His manifested presence. Their time together imparted a seed that took root in Wade.

Two years later, in 1958, the passion to build a "house of devotion" solely for ministering to the Lord began to grow rapidly in Wade until he prayed a pivotal prayer: **"Lord, if there could be a place where You could freely be who You want to be, and unhindered do what You want to do, I am fully available to You for this purpose."** He prayed it with an ache in his heart but not knowing how, when or where such a place could come to be.

In faith, Wade presented this availability to the Lord for the next decade while serving as a pastor and Bible teacher. Then in 1968 the Lord spoke clearly to Wade that the long-awaited vision would come to fruition on an old, run-down property called Pinecrest in Salisbury Center, NY. With a small team of dedicated supporters, much personal sacrifice and stretches of uncertainty, and a heart always ready to say

"Yes, Lord!" no matter the cost, the school was birthed. Pinecrest indeed became a house devoted to the Lord, a place well-known for being marked by God's abiding presence and used to raise up generations of lovers of Jesus.

I attended this school decades later, but that same presence and passion for intimacy with Christ remained. I went there hungry for more of God and left utterly drenched. The things Wade imparted during our precious times of prayer changed me forever. He carried a love for the secret place and walked in a depth that few enter into, yet somehow made this place of closeness with Jesus seem accessible. Wade showed us that the invitation to come up higher into God's glorious realm was open to all who would meet the conditions--mainly reckless abandonment and loving devotion to the Lord of Glory.

After leaving Pinecrest in 1998, Wade carried his vision for welcoming the fullness of God's manifest presence to the Washington D.C. region through Parousia Gatherings held in Virginia. The hunger for true face-to-face intimacy with Christ still burned white-hot in Wade until the very end; the last phone call I received from him, before he passed into Glory, showed Wade actively waiting before the Lord, seeking what was next for his journey with the Father.

Wade left a powerful legacy through his children (Ronald, Nancy, Bill, and Joanne), his life-changing books, and--most importantly-- through the thousands of lives impacted by his hunger for more of Jesus. The torch he carried was passed on to so many seeking divine visitation. I count it as a supreme honor to have been one so influenced and altered. My time with him in his home over the years and some trips together radically changed my life. Now more than three decades later after first meeting him, the fire Wade imparted still compels me into abandoned devotion unto the Christ of all Glory. The urgency to make way for the authority of the Lord to be established in the earth through a people set ablaze by His manifest presence still drives me because of my spiritual father's example.

I often wonder what words of wisdom Wade would speak to this current generation. Perhaps once again he would challenge hungry hearts with this simple invitation: "Come, be devoted unto the Lord. Make way for Him to have free reign that His glory may be manifested!" Or maybe he would remind us of the power of a single life utterly abandoned to Jesus' interests. Regardless, I know Wade would pour out whatever he could to see the Bride made ready for her Bridegroom.

As I reflect on my relationship with Wade Taylor, suddenly scenes from my years at Pinecrest flood my memory... long lines down that dorm hallway, eager faces expectant, simply wanting to spend a few precious moments with this dear father of the faith who walked so intimately with Jesus. I also have such joy when crossing paths with Wade's daughters at conferences. They share my tender memories of Pinecrest days gone by.

Yes, gratitude unto the Lord for allowing my life to intersect with such a true champion of intimacy with Christ. My friend Wade ran his race with endurance and kept extending his burning torch to all who drew near. The imprint he made shall ripple through generations yet to come. What a prize to pass on! As I reflect on the wealth of our inheritance through Wade Taylor, my heart cry rises higher, "Oh Lord, let me steward this holy legacy well!" I simply want to burn bright for Jesus, be a resting place for His presence, and walk ever closer with my Beloved just as my spiritual father modelled. Father hide us behind the cross that only you would be seen.

The message below **"Becoming the Tree of Life"** is one that is close to my heart. It was originally delivered by Wade at a small, intimate gathering in Avoca, New York before 1998. Of all the recordings I've listened to of Wade over the decades, this remains one of my favorites. After hearing it dozens of times, I finally had the message transcribed, then as editor carefully shaped it to retain Wade's unique tone and style in written form. Though I sought to preserve his voice, I shaped the transcript into a piece that could be absorbed and internalized in the quietness of private reading.

With appreciation and love,

Steve Porter

CHAPTER 1
BECOMING THE TREE OF LIFE

By Wade Taylor

The Progression of the Church: From Philadelphia to Laodicea. What I want to share is not to impress that I know something or to deliver a sermon. Rather, I am challenging myself, and you can listen in, because I am earnestly searching for something more in God and believe the Lord has something for us. What I will try to teach is something I am seeking for myself—I do not yet have it fully. So, I will write about something I need and do not completely possess. Please read on as I work up to it.

You are likely familiar with the seven churches described in Revelation. There seems to be a chronology, a progression from the book of Acts until the Laodicean church that spans history. There have always been parallels of all these churches in every generation. Yet there is also a progression. I believe we are in the last days, that Laodicea represents the last spiritual state of the church, and that there is a contrast between the Philadelphia church and the Laodicean church.

To Philadelphia, the Lord said they had a little power––at least it was lesser, but they had it nonetheless. But to Laodicea, He said this: **"Because thou sayest, I am rich, and increased with goods"** (Revelation 3:17). We live in the charismatic era of spiritual gifts and manifestations, a prosperity gospel of big churches—this pastor has two thousand, another four thousand, the next six thousand. All of this "because thou sayest." Both good and bad gifts and abilities, including finances, come because they proudly claim **to be rich** and increased in goods.

I believe the Lord is looking for something much more that can be deeply deposited within us. What He truly wants will function in individuals as He calls a people out of the lukewarm church. The visible church can be numbered, but the living church is Christ being formed in you. This church within the church (the remnant) cannot be numbered. The Lord spoke this to me: "I am moving away from the lukewarm Laodicean church into that which is represented by Philadelphia—a people who have 'a little strength' **with great opportunity**. The difference will be that my life can be found within [these believers] as the tree of life, rather than the dead forms men cling to because they say, 'I am rich and have need of nothing.'"

The Lord is calling us from that which represents Laodicea—enamored by gifts, position, title, finance, numbers—into a people in whom this deposit of "Christ in you" becomes functional. It will operate through a body of people—vessels through which the Lord manifests Himself as **the tree of life.**

This is what I am sensing and crying out for. I have some experience with spiritual gifts and activity, but there is something more. His spirit and life are meant to be found within us. I am not just seeking manifestations, but the living divine presence—the tree of life Himself being formed in a Body, in us!

Lord, form Yourself in us now. Make us suitable dwelling places for You. Move us from a "Laodicean" spirit that proudly relies on what we can generate into a dependency upon Christ being created in us. Out from us will flow rivers of living water. In Jesus's name, amen.

The Invisible, Mystical Body of Christ

That he might present it to himself <u>a glorious church</u>, <u>not having spot, or wrinkle</u>, or any such thing; but that it should be holy and without blemish (Ephesians 5:27).

Many preach that we cannot be at the end yet because Scripture says there must first be a church without spot or wrinkle, and that has not happened yet. But it has happened! There is already a church without spot or wrinkle, known only to God—two people here in this church, three there in that church, unknown to man but known to the Father as **the church within the church.**

The true church is the invisible, mystical, body of Christ. Its living stones are set in place by God's selection from among the raw material of the visible church. We look at the messy, visible church and say it is going nowhere, every program falls apart, nothing seems to happen. That is because the Lord is not after what man expects to see.

He is forming a seed that will be deposited in the "eternal" and spring up into new life. This seed taking form is the true church, known only to God. Those who see it this way are blessed, believing God is and rewards those who diligently seek Him. The Lord is not using a great visible work in our day, but rather He is preparing His bride instead to be His body with Christ as the head.

To Philadelphia, He said: **"These things saith he that is holy, he that is true, he that hath the key of David, he that openeth, and no man shutteth; and shutteth, and no man openeth...Behold, I have set before thee an open door, and no man can shut it...Thou hast a little strength [power]"** (Revelation 3:17-18). This word strength/power refers to a key—the ability to enter, to not be locked out.

Keys represent access and power. In Bible school, some strived hard to get certain keys because having keys meant status. But the key of David is different: it refers to a God-given ability to speak prophetically with creative authority, to release and see Zion (the true church) fully established. **It represents moving in God's power.**

This is still the Lord's way. Though we strive for impact in the visible, He is after a people in whom Christ is formed as life. Within us, He wants to manifest Himself as the tree of life described in Genesis and Revelation. It is Christ in us that overcomes and bears fruit, not ourselves. We are void without Him and His deeper work.

Ask the Lord to form Himself in you as **life.** Wait on Him to bring forth something eternal, not temporary. He longs to shape us into a dwelling place for Himself through which His life can flow. Amen.

The Power of Personal Impartation and Laying on of Hands

Now take a look at these verses:

"Wherefore I put thee in remembrance that thou stir up the gift of God, which is in thee by the putting on of my hands" (2 Timothy 1:6).

"Neglect not the gift that is in thee, which was given thee by prophecy, with the laying on of the hands of the presbytery" (1 Timothy 4:14).

You may ask, "What's this neglect, and where is it?" By faith, through the impartation of the Spirit by the working of the Word of God, there is in each and every one of us an operation, a gift, a manifestation of the Spirit. "Neglect not the gift that is in thee, which was given thee by prophecy, with the laying on of the hands of the presbytery" (1 Tim 4:14).

Now concerning laying on of hands. This is something that is accomplished personally and individually. I'll just give you a little example. I try to do some writing once in a while for our magazine *The Banner*. I'm not always too successful, and I've read a number of things that are written by others that are considered prolific and anointed. There are special authors that have a tremendous gift of writing.

A couple years ago, I was at a convention in North Carolina with about 2,000-3,000 people. A very famous minister and author was there speaking from the platform but was mobbed afterward and left quickly for his hotel. Around 10:30 that night as he headed back, I managed to stop him even though he didn't know me. I told him I was trying to do some writing and asked if he would pray, laying his hands on me. His first reaction was to rudely tell me off for bothering him after a tiring meeting when he just wanted to be left alone. But I persisted, probably coming across like the woman in Scripture who was willing to be called a dog if it meant getting her need met.

He started praying reluctantly, clearly annoyed to be bothered. But as he put his hands on me and began petitioning the Lord, suddenly the power of God profoundly hit him. When finished, amazed, he asked my name and where I was from, inviting me to his church to speak. He apologized profusely for his earlier rude reaction, startled by the intensity of the divine impartation. It was like a lightning bolt surged through both of us the moment he prayed. I experienced a tremendous transfer of anointing in those seconds. It was an absolutely profound impartation.

I haven't yet seen the full outworking of that impartation, as I still struggle to put pen to paper. Writing is difficult for me. But something was deposited into my being, at least in potential, that I believe will surface in the Lord's timing to break through limitations I've erected. There is a lack within myself that I acknowledge, but also this seed of divine impartation is lingering. As I come into a posture of faith, believing for a breakthrough while waiting on the Lord, not legalistically because I've put in a certain number of hours, but because I've touched the place of Spirit release within...from there, that which He imparted so subtly within me can begin to burst forth.

The laying on of hands is a one-to-one, personal type of ministry. This minister didn't mind speaking from the platform to thousands, but had I been part of a line of thousands wanting that touch from him, it would have drained life right out of him. This is why he was so disturbed by my request after already pouring out to the masses. Realistically there's no way he could have personally laid hands on every individual. I just happened to be the only one able to approach him about it afterwards.

This is exactly why I'm more comfortable and interested in smaller groups than large churches of thousands. A pastor of such a big congregation is forced to become an entertainer out of necessity. Within that size church are probably 25 leaders being held down who should have risen up to take responsibility for segments of the congregation. Real ministry implies personal, one-to-one contact through laying on of hands. There's no way a pastor can do that effectively with thousands of people. My thought is that those 25 subordinate leaders could shepherd small groups under the direction of the lead pastor rather than him feeling the weight of ministering to thousands alone every service. Laying on of hands requires personal ministry to each individual.

The impartation I received could have happened anywhere, it just happened to be 10:30 at night on a dark road by a motel. In those brief moments, something was implanted that has potential to impact thousands down the road, maybe more. I don't fully understand it yet, but I share this because I'm believing for that full release to not only surface within me but to become a means of impartation for others. My desire is that through my story, you would be stirred to embrace real ministry as these one-on-one times of laying on hands. Something profound and lasting happens in such personal encounters and transfers of anointing.

Each of you knows somebody——at least one person——who will listen when you talk. This means you have a "congregation"! It doesn't matter who it is; if someone will lend an ear, you can impart something from your life into theirs. There's no telling the potential ripple effect from there. What you share might impart something meaningful that this person passes on to someone else and so on, compounding to affect thousands down the road, all from a simple meaningful exchange in which you poured into one receptive soul.

The Compounding Effect of Simple, Personal Ministry

On the day we stand before the Lord, you'll be amazed at the cumulative effect you've had through simple person-to-person ministry. Real ministry is not defined by invitations to stand on platforms and impress crowds with entertaining speech. That is shallow thinking. True Kingdom impact comes through the personal impartations between individuals, often unseen, not the fleeting inspiration from a performance on a stage. When we stand before Jesus Christ, He will show us the compounding result of the seeds we planted in quiet moments through authentic relationship.

It's fine that big platforms can feed people and the Lord uses it, but it doesn't carry the depth and impact of real one-on-one ministry and impartation. What the Lord is truly after relates to person-to-person transferences of anointing––a laying on of hands where you personally pour something living from your life into another's. This may not be a formal prayer with literal hand-placement, but instead represents a contact through relationship where something transfers by the Spirit. Paul, a remarkable Apostle, recognized that true Kingdom ministry extended beyond addressing large gatherings, and included personal impartations to individuals like Timothy, his spiritual son. He said, **"Therefore, I remind you to rekindle the gift of God that is within you through the laying on of my hands"** (2 Tim. 1:6). This is intimate and personal––one life imparting into another life through an open channel that holy impartations can flow through.

I marvel that the Lord, having come to earth incarnated, looked ahead to establish a Church that would span history until swallowing up the nations in worship. Yet to launch this global, age-enduring organism, He chose only 12 insignificant people––not powerful, renowned leaders by worldly standards. If listing top candidates today, we'd name influential figures. But Jesus selected 12 absolute nobodies who in station and perceived ability were likely less than any individual reading this book. He only chose 12––not 12,000 or even 120, just 12––followers who the world would categorize as unimportant and lacking credentials. **<u>But these twelve became world-changers and history makers.</u>**

My friend, there are more than 12 that will read this book. Yet Jesus invested everything in just 12 seemingly "nobodies" with the hope and expectation they would turn the world upside down––**which they did!** They recognized the power and ability was not innate but from God

Himself. There was an impartation through relationship that equipped them for world-change.

Paul writes to "stir up the gift which is in thee...." What gift? I believe each person reading this can identify a time you were profoundly touched by God––not merely entertained, but *truly* ministered to in a life-transferring way. Through a message, a messenger, a divine encounter, the personalization of Christ has come to you by the Spirit's work.

In that instant, an impartation was made––God deposited something that lies within from that point on as a seed to be watered. We each were given a "talent". It may seem small or large based on perspective, but there is something there to now be stewarded and caused to grow and multiplied for greater purpose.

Now, concerning this gift, verses six and seven are tied together: **"Stir up the gift which is in thee by the putting on of my hands..."** (2 Tim 1:6). **"For God hath not given us the spirit of fear..."** (2 Tim 1:7). This spirit of fear relates directly to the tree of the knowledge of good and evil. Good––you'll be rewarded. Evil––you'll be punished. We have embraced a paradigm of good equals reward and bad equals punishment.

In normal Christian life and ministry, our relationship with God is based on this pendulum swing of good vs evil, reward vs punishment. We strive to be good out of motivation for blessing and avoid the bad to duck correction. If attentive in a service, reward. If apathetic, consequence. We vacillate between attempting to appease God through works while also fearful of displeasing Him if we don't appear spiritual enough.

Relating to God through the Tree of Life vs. Tree of Knowledge

For God hath not given us the spirit of fear; but of power, and of love, and of a sound mind (2 Timothy 1:7).

But Scripture says clearly, "God has not given us a spirit of fear." He wants to deliver us from relating to Him through the tree of the knowledge of good and evil, where we swing back and forth based on merit. I don't need to anxiously seek reward; God Himself is my reward! And when I stumble, "How much more shall your heavenly Father give good gifts to them that ask him?" (Mat 7:11). He is a good Father not waiting to punish, but longing to bless those who repent and love and obey Him.

God has not given us a spirit of fear, but of power, love, and soundness of mind. He is delivering us from relating to Him through the negative paradigm of the tree of knowledge of good and evil. Instead, He brings us to the tree of life––with Himself as the source––resulting in new creation authority, affection, and discipline.

Power here represents a recognition of our sonship identity. I am somebody in Christ––significance emanates from me through an expression containing divine substance. Empty hands have nothing to impart. But as I come to the tree of life, I receive spiritual deposits from God that become reserves I can release.

Before we can meaningfully impart into others, there must first be a deep working of God within ourselves. We each have this nagging voice constantly discrediting who we are, saying "You're nobody, you're less-than." But the Spirit is reshaping our self-perception, aligning it with how God sees us as His cherished sons and daughters. We are somebodies as new creations in Christ!

Embracing Our Identity as Sons and Daughters

Contrary to some teaching, a key step in advancing in God is starting to like yourself—fully accepting the person you are in Christ. I don't mean gaining ego or self-love, but embracing your identity as a loved son or daughter who contains precious deposits from God within. You are somebody! The tree of life bears 12 kinds of fruit for healing the nations. This speaks of the multi-faceted spiritual DNA within each of us that can nourish those around us. As we come to the river of life flowing from the throne, the trees lining it contain reserves of fruitful substance we can partake of for our replenishing and then giving out.

"In the midst of the street of it, and on either side of the river, was there the tree of life, which bare twelve manner of fruits, and yielded her fruit every month: and the leaves of the tree were for the healing of the nations" (Revelation 22:2).

Jesus prayed for oneness among believers, but the push for ecumenism and global unity is producing a counterfeit—an antichrist Babylon system. True unity is the spiritual, mystical church known to God, not external uniformity achieved through compromise.

As I discover who I am in Christ, God's power and light resides within me—more energy than an atomic bomb! I become a conduit where hungry hearts can tap into heavenly resources. Though that minister I mentioned previously wanted nothing to do with me in that moment, the instant he began praying, he became an open channel. Against his fleshly annoyance, the Spirit's power flowed through him into me.

Anyone with the right attitude about themselves can be used this way. When we put ourselves or others down, establishing a hierarchy, we inflict limitations. Using each other as stepping stones to lift ourselves up will result in cutting off the free flow of impartation. But as we come to the tree of life and embrace our identity in Christ, we have reserves within that can flow through us.

When we establish unhealthy comparison and limitation, it hinders the free flow of God's power. But as we come to the tree of life, we become conductors rather than resistors––open channels through which the Holy Spirit and life can flow bringing healing. The twelve kinds of fruit represent the positive, creative deposits of God within each of us as new creations. These reserves provide nourishment––life, strength, and sustenance––that others can freely draw from as they relate to us. But again, there first must be something deposited by God within us in order to have resources to impart.

The moment I become negative or express fear and death concerning my spirituality, I move back under the paradigm of the tree of knowledge of good and evil which God warned us not to touch as it leads only to death. Most of Christianity still functions in relating to God out of this harmful mindset rather than the life available through His new creation and intimacy with Christ.

Power reflects authorized access––like having keys to a car with potential energy locked up under the hood. Without the keys engaging that engine, the dormant power is useless to accomplish anything. We must take hold of the keys of the Kingdom that allows us to tap into resurrection power. Jesus said He has given us the keys, but we actually have to utilize them to unlock all that has been freely given to us in Him. As we grab hold of the keys of David (Revelation 3:17-18) ––the principles of intimate relationship––God's glory and power is manifested through us to change the world around us.

God established a covenant that He would relate to and move through a people. What He desires to accomplish in the earth, He chooses to do through human partnership, not apart from it. This covenant originated in Abraham, continued through generations, and culminates in union with Christ. He binds Himself to us and invites our cooperation to manifest His glory and power to the world around us!

Now, power simply means that I recognize the life of God, the ability of God, not my power, but His power. **"I am crucified with Christ:**

nevertheless, I live; yet not I, but Christ liveth in me" (Galatians 2:20). It's not my power, it's His power resident within me. I'm willing to become the conductor, the channel through which that power can flow out. In flowing out, it's going to manifest with the laying on of hands, which means I'm going to make myself personally available, one-to-one to impart. I've got to become conscious of impartation at work within my life. If I'm not conscious of impartation, if I become a sponge, trying to soak the life and light out of everybody else and drain them because I'm ever needing filled up, then I'm a receiver, not a giver. There's no opportunity to release something if my paradigm is one of lack. But as I come to the tree of life, I can contain reserves––the 12 manner of fruit––so others can freely receive as they relate to me.

I must recognize that through the laying on of hands there is spiritual impartation at work - and become a willing channel for God's power, not my own ("not I, but Christ liveth in me" - Gal. 2:20). My relationship with Jesus provides the reserve within to then release into others through personal ministry. Every believer knows at least one person willing to listen to them, if even for five minutes; that's an open door for holy impartation. I don't need a "big" ministry platform, just a willing heart before me. With this in mind comes a weighty responsibility and stewardship of my spiritual life to trust the Lord for something worthy to impart from my inner man unto others.

As I said beforehand there is no need to have a prominent ministry platform to impart something of value. All that's required is one willing listener. This truth brings a weighty stewardship over my spiritual life. I can trust God to produce something within worthy of imparting as I cultivate a right attitude toward Him and a right view of myself. Out of oneness with Christ, His life manifests through me to impact people. My relationship with Jesus provides the reserve to release. As I cultivate and allow God's deposits to increase within through time with Him, I'll have a greater measure to pour out. By abiding in intimacy with Him, I become a conduit where others can freely receive and be nourished.

Power relates to the understanding that there is something creative and positive within my life. I aim to move past the tree of knowledge of good and evil, settling once and for all that my focus is as steadfast as a flint towards Zion, towards God's purpose. Therefore, I am connected to the tree of life, choosing to believe in and impart life. I take on the characteristic of life, not death or the duality of good and evil, allowing life to operate and manifest within me. However, it's crucial to acknowledge that power can be lethal. For instance, Peter managed to cut off an ear, a perplexing action. This incident illustrates that if an ear is cut off, hearing becomes impossible. Yet, the Lord's action of restoring the ear signifies the power of healing and restoration.

The two-edged sword of God's Word rightly divides truth yet can also deeply wound when wrongly wielded. Many Christians have been left devastated by judgmental believers misusing Scripture. Without love governing its use, the Bible becomes a damaging weapon.

The Importance of Love Directing Power

Power must have love as its directing influence—agape that seeks the highest good of others, not selfish affection that discards people once it gets what it wants. That's fleshly human love masquerading to utilize people. Like a salesman saying, "I love you because you have something I want, but once I get it from you, I'll throw you away." The Lord's power flowing through us is meant to heal and restore; just as Jesus gently touched the ear Peter had impulsively cut off. Power and truth bring wholeness when handled with compassion.

God's love is sacrificial giving, not mutual benefit. "God so loved the world that He gave..." (John 3:16). Laying down your life for another through the laying on of hands is total surrender and outpour—not exchange. Jesus loved us unconditionally when there was nothing lovely or worthy in us that would draw His affection by human standards. But love sees hidden potential and calls it forth. God always acts in light of what could be unlocked in people, not just what presently appears.

So, for the power of God to flow through me, it must have love as its directing force to determine outcome rather than selfish desire. My walk with the Lord can't terminate with attaining spiritual gifts for my benefit. The goal must be capacity to impart the life of Christ into others––having reserves to pour out freely even as I was undeservedly poured into. Love motivates me beyond merely acquiring more for myself or to build up a name but to unlock spiritual treasures in those placed in my path. After receiving deposits from God by His love, love compels me to release those resources.

Power represents recognizing my relationship to the Lord and the life available through oneness with Him (the tree of life). Love serves as the motivation for how that power operates - directing how His deposits flow through me. This involves stewardship, choosing not to bury or merely consume the talents given to me, but to invest them freely through a willingness to impart to others. The fruit of the tree is truly "for the healing of the nations"––multitudes can be impacted through a single, surrendered life. As His power and love come into unity within me, I can be part of transforming communities and nations.

"For God hath not given us the spirit of fear; but of <u>power</u>, and of <u>love</u>, and of <u>a sound mind</u>" (2 Timothy 1:7).

The next word is **a sound mind**. By sound mind that doesn't mean being mental, it simply means that there's a discipline. That is, if I become a tree of life, and there comes within my life, fruit that can heal the nations, then the Lord has got to set me out in view before the nations where the needy person can come along and pluck some off. So that means I've got to be in the right place at the right time and the right attitude of mind to be there as a tree of life with fruit for the needy. This right attitude involves discipline.

The End of the Laodicean Church Age

Earlier, I referenced our transition away from the Laodicean Church Age. This era is concluding; it has reached its end, ceased, and is completed. The Lord is assembling a select group from the broader church community—a redeemed assembly of individuals being summoned from the dormant congregation. His glowing legacy, a bride brimming with intense passion. She represents a tree of life.

Not long ago, I received a letter from a woman who shared her journey with me. She recounted moving from Italy years ago and experiencing a profound spiritual awakening. She learned to read English through divine guidance and received numerous special revelations from the Lord. The letter, sent from Florida, described how she felt compelled by the Lord to share a particular insight about the Lord drawing a people unto Himself from amongst the church. She approached the pastor of a certain denomination to share her vision. Unfortunately, her efforts were met with resistance; the church swiftly excommunicated her, issuing a stern letter that formally expelled her from their community.

This response left her bewildered and disheartened. She was left wondering, "Did I do something wrong? What happened?" What she shared was profound and beautiful——a special revelation of an invisible church within a visible church, and the Lord calling the remnant church out to Himself, imparting an understanding and a revelation that the visible church didn't understand and didn't want because it interrupted their program. As a result, she was literally excommunicated.

So, I wrote her a letter and told her that she was really hearing correctly, and that she was to be complimented and encouraged. I looked up gatherings in the area that I felt had something of the Lord, and I encouraged her to get in touch with them. This sort of thing has been happening again and again, where the Lord is moving, yet His movement is not being received.

A sound mind implies discipline, which was notably absent during the charismatic movement. While there was an abundance of power, it lacked direction and focus, spreading thinly, and achieving little of substance. This dispensation led to the establishment of a materialistic kingdom rather than cultivating meaningful spiritual growth or impact. The gifts without fruit being manifested.

But the Lord is looking for a people who will properly steward His power, where there can be a lasting impartation through the laying on of hands, one to one. He desires the impartation of the substance of the eternal Kingdom of God and the life of God, so that it can be imparted to another––this substance, this life of God.

I deeply desire to cultivate this quality within myself, and through discipline, pass it on to others. If I, as one person, can share a fragment of God's heart with ten others, and do so in a way that they grasp the significance of what has transpired, each of them could then impart that understanding to ten more. Imagine sitting down with a piece of paper and mapping out this process, with each of those ten sharing a part of that experience with ten additional people.

Before long, the kingdoms of this world would become the **Kingdoms of our Lord**, and something significant would be accomplished. It can all happen. That's why the Lord started with 12 people. He imparted that concept to them, and they, in turn, imparted it to others. Literally, in one generation, they turned the world upside down.

"Is it such a fast that I have chosen? A day for a man to afflict his soul? Is it to bow down his head as a bulrush, and to spread sackcloth and ashes under him? Wilt thou call this a fast, and an acceptable day to the Lord?" (Isaiah 58:5).

Isaiah 58:5 resonates with the message I've been sharing. It questions the nature of true fasting and what constitutes an acceptable day to the Lord. This verse speaks to the essence of internal spirituality, where many are becoming recipients akin to the tree of the knowledge of good and evil. The Lord suggests moving beyond mere actions to the laying on of hands, to impartation, transforming me into a giver. Like the tree of life bearing 12 kinds of fruit for the healing of the nations, there's something within me ready to be shared with others.

Verse six states, **"Is not this the fast that I have chosen: to loose the bands of wickedness, to undo the heavy burdens, to let the oppressed go free, and to break every yoke? Is it not to share your bread with the hungry, and that you bring to your house the poor who are cast out; when you see the naked, that you cover him, and not hide yourself from your own flesh?"** This verse speaks of a profound promise. If this one verse operated in my life, it would be absolutely transformative.

It also reads in Isaiah 58:8-9, **"Then your light shall break forth like the morning, your healing shall spring forth speedily, and your righteousness shall go before you; the glory of the Lord shall be your rear guard. Then you shall call, and the Lord will answer; you shall cry, and He will say, 'Here I am.'"**

The verse continues in Isaiah 58:9b-11, **"If you take away the yoke from your midst, the pointing of the finger, and speaking wickedness, if you extend your soul to the hungry and satisfy the afflicted soul, then your light shall dawn in the darkness, and your darkness shall be as the noonday. The Lord will guide you continually, and satisfy your soul in drought, and strengthen your bones; you shall be like a watered garden, and like a spring of water, whose waters do not fail."**

Prayer for Transformation and Fruitfulness

For a long time, we have tried to be spiritual and religious, relating to the tree of knowledge of good and evil. *But today, Lord, you're calling us to something more––to life, to the tree of life, to a relationship, to oneness with you. May you, Lord, come within our lives, and may we become a source of life, a spring, Lord, that we may become the tree of life, and that the fruit thereof may be made available to others through the laying on of our hands.*

There will be an impartation for the healing of the nations, *Lord, that our attitude can be such that we will see healing and restoration in life! Change us, Lord; bring about that love and discipline, Lord, that there may be a flow of your power that's been restrained for so long, pent up and held back because you haven't had that conductor of life through which your power could flow forth in the laying on of hands.*

Lord, bring that love and discipline to our lives, that we will function in love and discipline, in the impartation of life, healing, and restoration, that we can, Lord, fulfil what you're speaking in this profound chapter of Isaiah, which applies to each one of us.

Now, Lord, enable us to hear that which I said in the beginning. I need this within my life. I desperately need it, Lord, desperately within my life. I'm asking, Lord, for that working of your Spirit, where there may be fruit, where there may be that power operating, Lord, in a very creative way from my life, that there will be signs following, and not just some flowery word to entertain or to show forth my own spirituality in some dismal way.

But Lord, there can be that impartation of life, where there can be literally an impartation in the sense that hands have been laid upon another, life has been deposited, and there's that which is creative that shall come forth.

Now, Lord, we hold all this before you, that it will become a creative word, accomplishing the higher purpose for which you have sent it. We thank you, Lord, and we give you the glory. In Jesus' name. Amen and Amen.

Message Outline of Wade Taylor's - "Becoming the Tree of Life"

For those that desire to teach this message to others

I. Introduction

1. Challenging himself and the listeners to seek something more in God
2. Not preaching to impress but seeking this deeper experience himself

II. The Progression of the Church: From Philadelphia to Laodicea

1. Contrast between the Philadelphia church ("little strength") and Laodicean church ("rich, have need of nothing")
2. God is calling people out of lukewarm Laodicea to have His life within as the tree of life

III. The Invisible, Mystical Body of Christ

1. The true church is invisible, known only to God, being formed as a seed
2. God is preparing a bride, a body with Christ as head, not focused on visible works

IV. The Power of Personal Impartation and Laying on of Hands

1. Biblical examples of impartation through laying on of hands (2 Tim 1:6, 1 Tim 4:14)
2. Author's personal experience receiving an impartation from a well-known minister
3. Real ministry happens through personal one-on-one impartations, not just platform speaking
4. The compounding effect of simple person-to-person ministry over time

V. Relating to God through the Tree of Life vs. Tree of Knowledge

1. Getting free from fear-based relating to God through reward/punishment (tree of knowledge)

2. Receiving power, love and a sound mind by relating through the tree of life

3. Power - recognizing our identity and spiritual authority as sons/daughters

4. Love - having reserves deposited by God to impart to others

5. Sound mind - discipline to be a yielded channel for God's power to flow through

VI. The End of the Laodicean Church Age

- God is calling out a remnant passionate bride from the Laodicean church

1. Example of woman excommunicated for sharing this revelation

2. Need for discipline to steward God's power rightly, not just seeking manifestations

3. VII. Conclusion

4. Prayer for transformation to become sources of life who impart through laying on of hands

5. Desperate need for this working of the Spirit to bear lasting fruit through our lives

So in summary, the key theme is progressing from lukewarm, superficial Laodicean spirituality to becoming a source of divine life and impartation to others by relating to God through the tree of life. This requires personal encounters with God's power, being motivated by love, and embracing discipline to be a yielded vessel.

Here are 50 thought-provoking questions for small groups and private study.

1. What does it mean to move from a "Laodicean" spirit to a "Philadelphia" spirit in the church today?
2. How can we nurture "Christ being formed in you" rather than pursuing superficial measures of success?
3. What would it look like for God's life to manifest "as the tree of life" in believers today?
4. Are we seeking spiritual manifestations or the living presence and formation of Christ in us?
5. How can we transition from pride and self-reliance to dependency on Christ in us?
6. What gifts and talents has God deposited in you for impartation to others?
7. Are you actively stirring up and stewarding the gifts God has placed in you?
8. How can we move from performing to intimate spiritual impartation?
9. Do you see yourself as having a congregation of even just one to impart to?
10. How can the cumulative impact of personal ministry surpass platform performance?
11. Are you embracing your identity or living hindered by self-limiting beliefs?
12. How can we nurture spiritual fruit instead of just entertaining people?
13. What key of authority or access has God provided for you?
14. In what ways do we still minister blessing and cursing, punishment and reward?
15. How can we transition from dualistic thinking to embracing the tree of life?
16. Are you actively imparting or merely receiving from others?

17. How can the body of Christ become a conductor of God's life rather than resistance?
18. What aspects of the deeper life in God are you feeling after and crying out for?
19. How can we move from sterile religion to intimate relationship and oneness with Christ?
20. What disciplined cultivation is required for you to impart spiritual fruit?
21. Do you see the invisible church emerging amidst struggling systems?
22. Are you embracing a "little strength" mindset over seeking bigness?
23. How can we steward God-given authority for building rather than destruction?
24. In what ways have you experienced legalism versus grace and empowerment?
25. What would it look like to walk in the vitality of the tree of life rather than traditions that leave us dead?
26. How can we live as conduits of God's life rather than showcasing our own talents?
27. What passions has God placed in your heart to impart to the world around you?
28. Do you feel equipped for spiritual parenthood - releasing an inheritance to the next generation?
29. What disciplined cultivation is needed for you to bear lasting spiritual fruit?
30. Are you embracing humility and faithfulness over a drive for expanding influence?
31. Do you depend deeply on union with Christ to the point that His life flows out of you?
32. How can we steward influence faithfully without succumbing to pride?
33. What gifts has God cultivated in you or placed in you recently?

34. How do you discern between living by God's power versus your own strength?

35. Do you think of yourself as one still in need of transformation or one who has fully arrived?

36. How can we nurture spiritual life in others from a position of humble dependence rather than superficial strength?

37. What might it look like to have the "key of David" operating in the church today?

38. Do you feel your spiritual tank is full or in need of being replenished?

39. Who is God bringing across your path for you to impart to?

40. What disciplines or cultivations might prepare you for greater spiritual impartation?

41. How is God stirring your heart to move from maintenance to bold impartation?

42. Where do you see spiritual fruit ripening in your life, ready to be shared with others?

43. What limitations or weaknesses is God calling you to surrender?

44. How can we embrace the cross daily so that resurrection life flows through our hands?

45. Do you gravitate more toward receiving affirmation or imparting without recognition?

46. Whose spiritual parenting played a key role in your formation?

47. What would you identify as your core spiritual gifts ready to be shared?

48. How can we stay vitally connected to the True Vine amid busy schedules?

49. Who around you is hungry for the spiritual fruit you carry?

50. How can we practically move from fruitless religion to the vibrant life of the Spirit?

Echoes of Devotion:
The Spiritual Journey of John Wright Follette

"But seek first his kingdom and his righteousness, and all these things will be given to you as well" – (Matthew 6:33).

John Wright Follette, a remarkable figure whose life journey was characterized by devotion, creativity, and spiritual insight, was born on October 30, 1883, in New Paltz, New York. His story is not just a narrative of dates and events but a tapestry woven with the threads of spiritual substance, faith, and a deep intimacy with the Lord.

From an early age, Follette showed an inclination towards the spiritual aspects of life. He was captivated by the presence of Jesus Christ and dedicated himself to following Him with all his heart. This dedication took various forms – he was not just a devout follower but also a teacher, singer, musician, preacher, artist, and poet. His multifaceted talents were an expression of his deep love for the Lord and served as channels through which he communicated his faith.

Follette's journey as a spiritual teacher began in the early 1900s, a time of significant religious revival in America. He was both a recipient and an active participant in the outpourings of the Holy Spirit, witnessing firsthand the ebbs and flows of spiritual movements across the country. His keen observations and experiences led him to offer cautionary advice about the pursuit of Biblical promises and signs, which, while not always well-received at the time, later proved to be insightful and valuable.

Family roots played a significant role in Follette's life. His lineage traced back to the Huguenots, French Protestants who faced persecution and eventually found refuge in America. This heritage instilled in him a deep appreciation for religious freedom and a strong Protestant faith. His upbringing in a devout family in New Paltz, where he was immersed in nature and spiritual teachings, laid the foundation for his future ministry.

Follette's education was diverse and comprehensive. He studied at the New York Normal School in New Paltz, Drew Theological Seminary, and Taylor University. His academic pursuits were not limited to theological studies; they also included music and the arts, reflecting his belief in the interconnectedness of all forms of worship and expression.

His teaching career was significant, especially his time at the Rochester Bible Training School and later at the Southern California Bible School. Follette was more than just a teacher; he was a mentor and spiritual father, deeply impacting the lives of his students. Wade Taylor was one such student who spent time alone with Follette in his home. Wade once remarked that if you went to John Wright Follette's house and stayed with him for one week - even if he spoke no words to you - your life would still be absolutely transformed just from watching his deep walk with the Lord. Even simple moments, like how Follette would often place a plate and coffee cup for the Lord as he welcomed Him to sit with him during meals, were deeply touching. His classes were not just academic sessions but spiritual experiences, where he combined doctrinal teachings with practical life lessons and deeper insights that had a profound effect on those around him.

Follette's writings and poetry are a testament to his profound spiritual insights and artistic talent. His works, including "Smoking Flax" and "Broken Bread", are not mere literary pieces but reflections of a life lived in close communion with God. They continue to inspire and guide believers, offering a refreshing perspective on the Christian faith.

Despite his numerous contributions and a life of service, Follette remained a humble servant, never seeking personal glory but always pointing others to Christ. His legacy is not just in his writings or teachings but in the lives he touched and the spiritual truths he imparted.

In conclusion, John Wright Follette was a deep man of God whose life was a beautiful blend of creativity, devotion, and wisdom. His story inspires us to pursue a deeper relationship with God, to use our talents for His glory, and to live a life of obedience and faith. His legacy continues to live on, guiding and inspiring generations of believers to walk a path of spiritual depth and authenticity.

CHAPTER 2
TROUBLE - A SERVANT FOR SPIRITUAL GROWTH

By John Wright Follette

Did you ever test yourself as to how you react to trouble or tragedy? In life's school we often find that God uses trouble or misfortune to prove our faith or to test our character. Trouble has a way of stalking down the road and meeting us so many times when we least expect it.

I am sure we all know that such proving or testing may befall us without our being personally or directly the cause of it. Many, many times it is beyond our control. If it were otherwise we should probably avoid all such testings and keep to an easy, smooth path. But we should remember that trouble, as well as the hours of sunshine and music, is a part of the divine arrangement and has a place in our program. Trouble and severe testings are not necessarily a sign of sin, failure, or lack of spirituality. They are often a sign of spirituality and growth which God must test and prove, for we are His workmanship.

Many people have the notion that the life of the Christian is, or should be somewhat charmed, void of trouble, testing, tribulation and suffering. Such people have shaped up for themselves, or hold as an ideal of real Christian living, au impossible or unscriptural conception as an objective.

Where in the world such people, so bewitched, have been living all these years, or what books they have read, is beyond me! Surely they do not know history, Christian experience or the Bible. For all these keep ever before us the truth that *"Man is born unto trouble, as the sparks fly upward"* (Job 5:7). *"Many are the afflictions of the righteous but the Lord delivered him out of them all"* (Psa. 34:19). *"For our light affliction, which is but for a moment, worketh for us a far more exceeding and eternal weight of glory"* (2 Cor. 4:17). *"Yea, and all that will live godly in Christ Jesus shall suffer persecution"* (2 Tim. 3:12). *"In the world ye shall have tribulation: but be of good cheer; I have overcome the world"* (John 16:33). *"And not only so, but we glory in tribulations also: knowing that tribulation worketh patience"* (Rom. 5:3).

Surely on the basis of all these Scriptures, we as Christians know better than to pray for exemption from trouble, and since we know that in God's plan it is a part of our inheritance, let us not avoid its peculiar ministry.

History is replete with examples of lives wrecked because of ungraceful reaction to trouble. In spite of the accumulated experiences of the ages, and the wisdom and the philosophy of the seers, many still fail to recognize that behind her mask, trouble is a *servant* to assist us. Any other view is due to lack of vision and perspective in that range. Too many see the immediate, the local, and interpret life and relative questions from a circumscribed viewpoint. The Scriptures say, "*While we look not at the things which are seen.*"

As Christians, after we are convinced in our hearts that trouble is not designed to defeat us, is not a mere nuisance or cruelty, but is one of the corrective elements in great living, we must needs learn how to use it. How many problems would be solved and shipwrecks of faith be avoided could we take a positive, constructive attitude and see that trouble is one of the agents and mighty instruments placed in our hands for the shaping of character and the releasing of potential power for correct and glorious building! How do you use trouble? Naturally, because of physical and fundamental elements in our make-up, we shun pain, discomfort and trouble. But that is because we relate them purely to their action upon the physical or upon the present mood. Many times hours are spent in praying away trouble, the great servant. At times we take long, circuitous journeys to avoid meeting her. Finally, when we are compelled to meet her, we spend a long, long time telling her or God that we do not like her and we wonder and wonder why we ever had to meet her. But trouble is not to be reasoned with; she is utterly unreasonable. She is to be *used*.

Please disabuse your minds of the erroneous thought that if you are good or a real spiritual Christian, totally yielded and consecrated, your life is therefore to be a charmed one and that God will spare you from trouble or disappointment. No, to reach such a fine place of consecration and yieldedness is only to make you a fit candidate for tribulation.

Tribulation is a word God uses in relation to saints. The etymology of the word means *threshing*. The farmer does not thresh weeds; he threshes the golden wheat that the grain may be separated *from* the chaff and the sticks. He is after grain, not trying to pound out some straw. Therefore God says, *Tribulation worketh patience;* that is, the golden grain of patience, long-suffering and kindness, comes by way of threshing or tribulation. Think of the splendid spiritual grain of character and noble living produced only through the tribulation process. The spiritual tone and quality of the mighty men of God came only through trouble and suffering.

In the world about us, in the fields of fine music, art and literature, the artist never reaches the climax of his labors and gives to the world the best in creative beauty and strength until he has known the poignant touch of personal sorrow or grief or trouble. Oftentimes it is like a divine alchemy turning the ordinary and prosaic life into a glorious display of divine power, fortitude and beauty. It is the *use* of trouble that releases the deeper springs of our lives and sets allow the streams of mercy and understanding which a perishing world needs.

Do not misunderstand me; I am not saying that trouble alone makes us strong or noble or that it alone has a transforming power. I am dealing with you as Christians who believe Romans 8:28, and that text, as you see, is never to be applied to lives which are not surrendered. That is why many unsaved people never understand the outworking of the Scriptures in the daily walk, but if the Christian has anything remotely approaching the Spirit of Christ, he can make trouble a servant to bring forth the best in him. This I suggest in my poem, *Trouble Is a Servant.*

But trouble in itself is neutral or passive; the whole matter depends upon *how* we use it. One may take an inactive attitude and lose the benefit of the trial; justify himself, and trouble will make him bitter or resentful, or it can make him hard, cruel and cynical. People who have no faith, no perspective of thought or vision, let trouble do all sorts of harmful and cruel things to them, but thanks be to God there are many wonderful people upon whom trouble has fallen who were able to see and to discern behind its mask a servant at their beck and call, to build them lives of strength and beauty.

In a simple study of such lives we find a certain creative power which makes out of their calamity a magnificent privilege. You have noticed in lives a twofold reaction to trouble or tragedy: either it will break us in spirit, melting the hardness and bringing us in our helplessness to God, or it will throw us upon our feeble resources and human reasonings, and this in turn at times hardens us in spirit, makes us critical and often cynical. It robs the heart of the great privilege of trusting God and the developing of the life into rich and helpful avenues.

Trouble will make you either *bitter* or *better.* Notice how very much alike these words are, and how very little is needed to change them; just the letter "I." Yes, dear ones. it is the "I" that changes the whole matter. When the "I" keeps out of the question, out of the difficulty, life will *be better;* but when the "I" is introduced and we get mixed in the trouble, life will become bitter and we hard. Too many times this "I" gets in the way; the poor, little, hurt ego gets a slap and down the street he runs, screaming for attention. The dear little ego sits in his doorway and weeps tears of self-pity until his eyes are so red and inflamed that he just cannot see things as they are or should be.

It takes a quiet heart, peace of spirit, and clear vision (long range, if you please), to interpret trouble in terms of strength and high living. Little souls, small people, are usually hurt all the time; the *ego* within is unduly important and consequently is easily hurt or flattered. Such souls have too small a world and hence everything relates directly to the self within. They will have a very difficult time, to say the least.

Frequently such souls are persons who are seeking justice, fairness, and a proper adjustment of life. They never seem to learn. We are not here for justice; we are here to live. If you expect to be a spiritual and victorious Christian, you may as well learn here and now to drop justice out of your vocabulary as far as it may relate to your life. We do not get justice now. God's Saturday night of settlement has not yet come.

Some live as though life and the Christian experience were some kind of slot machine: you put in a dime's worth of kindness and pull out three yards of blessing; then five cents' worth of charity and you think God must bless you next Saturday night. Be very good, kind or generous and next week the winds will blow you a fortune. It is true that what we sow that shall we also reap, and bread cast upon the waters shall return, but God is not too clear on the time element. So we shall not always receive our justice here and now.

Jesus never taught His followers to expect justice. Paul did not receive justice. Even great leaders in history did not always receive justice here and now. Do not mistake me; I do not me. an that the Christian or the spiritually-minded one is not conscious of the hurt or the trouble of the injustice. Believe me, dear souls, the Holy Spirit makes one all the more sensitive to the pain, the hurt and the wrong, but the victorious soul has found the gift of grace and the love of God sufficient to hinder the trouble from marring his spirit.

The closer one gets to Christ the more sensitive he will be to pain, to little, petty, mean ways and all the train of unkind and unlovely things which would vex the heart and tarnish the spirit. The eyes are now anointed and he sees in them privileges of overcoming and high living. I am sure we have all lived long enough to have had some injustice done us. Yet today God has given us grace not to harbor any resentment or hard feelings. To have trouble or injustice and *know* the feeling of it, and yet live above and far from its damaging power, is a sign of real spirituality, a sign of Christian character He has wrought in the life.

Someone learned of a real *injustice* done me in material things one time, and he was horrified to know it came from a Christian source. Such treatment as that," he said, "*is* absolutely wrong. I would not stand for it." Of course it was wrong and very unfair, and at times I was amazed and tried, but I kept my heart and life open for justice and the right thing to be done by me; however, I was neglected and seemingly forgotten. But God had taken me quite a long distance on the road and I knew He would take care of the matter; so I took of His grace and love and stood it. It never caused me a resentful spirit, nor did I allow the hurt and the disappointment to fester into a sore. And today I praise God for the realities of His life in my heart to keep it sweet when trouble and unfair dealings would chill it to indifference and hardness.

Had we time we could trace through history, both sacred and secular, scores of noble men and women who were *not* spared the hard places in life. They were good, moral, kind, noble, and yet came under the disciplinary measures of trouble. Certainly Paul knew trouble or he never could have written, *"In labors more abundant, in stripes above measure, in prisons more frequent, in deaths oft. Of the Jews five times received I forty stripes save one. Thrice was I beaten with rods, once was I stoned, thrice I suffered shipwreck"* (2 Cor. 11:23-25). Yet out of it all he comes purified and strengthened, a noble expression of God's grace and an example for the ages to come that trouble may be used to build a Christian character.

In the Old Testament we find Joseph and Job and many others demonstrating the same truth. Surely Joseph might have said, "All these things are against me. Where is God? Why all this confusion and trouble when He promised me great victory and triumph?" Yet listen to him after in faith he comes through, *"But as for you, ye thought evil against me; but God meant it unto good"* (Gen. 50:20). We are following in the steps of Christ, who said that the servant was not above his lord. And we read of Him, *"Though he were a Son, yet learned he obedience by the things which he suffered."*

What are you seeking in your trouble today? Is it *deliverance* or *development?* You may have the one and not grow, or you may have both and grow. Get the development first and the deliverance will be yours, too. Let this servant minister to you in a way no other servant can. Take the positive attitude and use your trouble as one of the most skillful and wonderful instruments God ever placed into your hands for the working out of the character of Christ to be duplicated in you.

Trouble, if correctly used, will bring you great peace and a deep surrender of spirit which nothing else can work in you. I have not gone far on the way but I can give as my personal testimony that these deeper revelations of truth and clear understanding of the things of God have come only through suffering. I cannot offer you any other method. May God grant you grace to take your share of trouble. Don't pray for exemption, but may He teach you and use this strange servant to build your life into noble proportions of strength and beauty, and from your life healing streams of understanding and love will flow to broken lives and timid, fearful hearts "*For* he who suffers most has most to give."

Outline of John Wright Follette's
"Trouble - A Servant for Spiritual Growth"

I. Introduction

    A. Testing our reaction to trouble or tragedy

    B. Trouble as part of the divine arrangement and a sign of spirituality and growth

II. The misconception of a charmed Christian life

    A. The notion of a trouble-free Christian life

    B. Biblical examples of trouble and tribulation in the lives of the righteous

III. The purpose of trouble in God's plan

    A. Trouble as a corrective element in great living

    B. The need to learn how to use trouble constructively

IV. The role of trouble in shaping character and releasing potential

    A. The importance of a positive, constructive attitude towards trouble

    B. The dangers of avoiding or complaining about trouble

V. Tribulation as a process for saints

    A. The etymology and meaning of tribulation

    B. The spiritual grain of character produced through tribulation

VI. The creative power of trouble in the lives of artists and Christians

    A. The transformative effect of personal sorrow, grief, or trouble

    B. The release of deeper springs of life through trouble

VII. The neutral nature of trouble and the importance of our response

    A. The twofold reaction to trouble: breaking or hardening the spirit

    B. The role of the "I" in determining the outcome of trouble

VIII. The Christian's attitude towards justice and fairness

   A. The need to drop the expectation of justice in this life

   B. The sufficiency of God's grace and love in the face of injustice

IX. The increased sensitivity to pain and injustice as one grows closer to Christ

   A. The anointing of the eyes to see privileges of overcoming and high living

   B. The sign of real spirituality in living above the damaging power of trouble

X. Examples of noble men and women who faced trouble

   A. Biblical examples: Paul, Joseph, and Job

   B. The importance of seeking development over deliverance in times of trouble

XI. Conclusion

   A. The positive attitude and use of trouble as a skillful instrument for growth

   B. The peace, surrender, and deeper revelations that come through suffering

THE CALL OF DEEP UNTO DEEP

By John Wright Follette

Down in the depth of my nature

Where the issues of life are born,

From that unknown mystical realm,

Surviving through ages of storm,

A call is forever rising—

But its language I cannot speak.

It was born ere I had being,

'Tis the call of deep unto deep.

Our mother tongue here is awkward,

For no words can fully express

The needs in the depths of nature,

In bondage to sin and distress.

Our hearts in their depths sorely ache;

They hunger; they call; and they seek—

Then silently wait an answer

To the call of deep unto deep.

Down deep in the heart of our God,

In mystical regions sublime,

In the Godhead's holy council

Long before our world or our time,

An answer was fully prepared

Every pain, every ache to meet,

In Christ, God's only begotten,

Is answer to deep unto deep.

The Answer indeed was the Word,

The Word when expressed was the Son.

Oh language of God how profound!

In answer what more could be done?

The heart of our God is hungry,

His portion, His people to seek.

"I thirst," was cried by the Answer—

'Tis the call of deep unto deep.

Echoes Of The Deep

John Wright Follette

"Deep calleth unto deep at the noise (call) *of thy water-spouts: all thy waves and thy billows are gone over me.*" Psalm 42:7.

Although this Psalm is not purely Messianic we find in verse seven a most impressive and suggestive prophecy of Christ in His work of redemption. The picture is that of the boundless ocean evidently in great commotion. It is storm-swept. Its waves are lashed into fury and as they heave and rock, the wind sweeps down and whirls the water into gigantic waterspouts thus discovering deep vacuums which yawn and, as it were, call one to another. Into the midst of this awful confusion and wild fury a helpless soul is cast and while the waves and billows sweep over and over him, his voice is raised in agony. Mingled with the boom and roar of the storm we hear him call out, *"Deep calleth unto deep at the noise of thy waterspouts: all thy waves and thy billows are gone over me."*

Here is another interpretation, mentioned by the Editor of Elbethel, which is very suggestive and helpful. She shows how *deep calling unto deep* represents one unknown *depth of need* in our hearts moved upon by God and calling to another. This is so true. As he moves upon one "deep" in nature it calls for movement upon another and thus is God doing a deepening work in the hearts and lives of His children today. The waterspouts are means used by God in this wonderful work. His ways are not pleasing to the natural but are most effectual when permitted to work out His purpose for us.

One day the Lord brought this verse to my attention with still another application and lesson. It was soon after visiting the Grand Canyon in Arizona and I think for that reason it spoke with freshness of meaning. It was there that the significance of *depth* dawned upon my natural sense. I believe this canyon is considered the most sublime of all earthly spectacles. Even a most superficial description of the enormous abyss may hardly be put into words.

Standing upon the rim one overlooks a thousand square miles of pyramids and minarets, carved from painted depths. Many miles away and more than a mite below his feet, the tourist sees a tiny silver thread which he knows to be the giant Colorado. Imagine a stupendous chasm, in places from ten to thirteen miles wide from rim to rim, more than two hundred miles long in all of its meanderings, and more than a mile deep! I shall not presume to tell of its mysterious beauty—strange and unearthly. It is never the same. The colors change with every changing hour; it is ever undergoing transformation. The lights and shades, mists, filmy rainbow veils, cloud fleeces, and purple shadows all move in perfect harmony of mass and color.

It quite outstretches the faculty of measurement. At times it is a brooding, terrible thing, unflinchingly real, yet spectral as a dream. I only mention the Canyon because to my own heart and mind it gave me fresh apprehension of *depth—but* depth only in the natural.

THE FIRST DEEP

Now let us turn to the meaning of our text as it came to my heart after seeing something of such majestic heights and depths. *Deep calleth unto deep*! The first deep mentioned, speaks of the unutterable and fathomless depths of the human heart. It is that mysterious, subtle, under-region or ocean floor of man's heart. In the natural he moves about upon the surface and only occasionally is aware of its hidden possibilities. In Proverbs 4:23 we find it is the source from which are the issues of life. It is not the place of manifestation and actual expression, but where issues are born which in time find their way to the surface and come into notice. It is that desperate need incurred by the sin and fall of the whole race in Adam.

What is the character of this strange deep? What could be the *nature* of such an unexplored and foreboding region? Jeremiah 17:9 tells us it is *deceitful above all things, and desperately wicked.* Jeremiah, even though a prophet, was baffled at the thought of sounding it or telling in detail its workings. It was enough in his estimation to say as he did in the original, "*It* is desperately sick and incurable." Then he adds, *Who can know it?*

Dear friends, we may perhaps measure the Grand Canyon and with the scientific instruments of today sound its depth and magnificent dimensions. We are appalled and silenced before such majestic workings of God. Our feeble sense of distance even here is too weak to comprehend—and this is but a little of His handiwork. Could we measure the *deep* mentioned in the text? No apparatus, however ingeniously constructed, ever finds the hidden springs of the human heart. Thank God, it is not given man to know. Pie has nowhere told us to try so impossible and dispiriting a task.

To begin with, man has not the correct estimation of distance in regard to the depth mentioned here, neither has the honesty of heart to read truthfully even the few feet which at times he finds open to his gaze. My heart takes courage to know there is One who does know. There is One who is able to descend down, down, down, even to the bottom of the heart and there discern the need in all its details, of sin, pain, agony, misery, and want. Such work is left to Him. I am not called upon to venture down into such a hazardous pit. In 1 Chronicles 28:9 we find that "*The Lord searcheth all hearts and understandeth* all *the imaginations of the thoughts.*" We find the same truth in Psalm 44:20, 21: "*If we have forgotten the name of our God, or stretched out our hands to a strange god; Shall not God search this out? for He knoweth the secrets of the heart.*" In Psalm 139:1, 2, we find David's testimony: "*O Lord, thou hast searched me and known me. Thou knowest my downsitting and mine uprising, thou understandest my thoughts afar off.*"

Then in the same Psalm David prays, "*Search me, O God, and know my heart; try me and know my thoughts.*" Do you think he prayed this before he had discovered the first shadows and the clouds of darkness over the rim of his own heart? I believe he prayed it *after* he had been convinced in his own soul that *he* was not equal to it and no doubt feared the depths hidden there. So in faith and courage (it takes courage) he prayed that God might do the searching.

Maybe some of us have been searching, and feebly and tremblingly trying to descend into this unspeakable and dingy deep, crowded with shadows, mist and haunting sounds. I dare say that all, at times, have ventured over the rim and really meant it as a pious act to convince our hearts that (out of Christ) we are hopelessly undone and altogether miserable. Pungent conviction of the Holy Ghost is most wholesome and conducive to spiritual growth. But I have never yet met a Christian who tried (alone) to descend those depths but that he ended in hopeless, morbid, introspection; and his faith failing him, he became self-centered.

Since God has told us that such work belongs to Him, let us not try to become holier or deeper in God by unnecessary and uncalled for self-humiliation. There are in this *deep* hidden things—sin, pride, duplicity, unbroken-ness, unyieldedness, self-complacency, weakness, and fear. Only God knows all the unutterable possibilities. Were it not for the grace of God and the life of Jesus, where would any of us be today? I am a firm believer in the total depravity of the natural man. I believe the *deep of* need found in the human heart (even in each one) holds the possibilities of any sin, no matter how heinous, were one to be placed in an environment needed to foster its growth and the power of the Blood and restraining influence of the Holy Spirit lifted.

This is surely not a pleasant picture. No one delights in rehearsing the failures of the old creation. I mention it only because it is truth, and to rejoice with my fellow-Christians in the revelation of Christ as the mighty Deliverer. Some are afraid we may not know the deformity and desperate need found in this first *deep* mentioned. They ask if this question is not to be dealt with. Yes, friends, this *deep* is to be considered; hut with more adequate skill and intelligence of mind than we have. As Christians we now have the mighty Holy Spirit to do this very work for as. Romans 8:27—"*And He that searcheth the hearts knoweth what is the mind of the Spirit, because He maketh intercession for the saints according to the will of God.*"

I believe that the blessed Holy Spirit, as part of His ministry, comes as a mighty Intercessor for us in behalf of the deep need found in us. We are persuaded that we are unable to cope with it. Only failure and God's grace can bring us to such a commendable position. Then He comes in, and moves down, down, down into those hidden caverns, down into the crevices, and breathless depths, down upon the ocean floor of this unknown deep. There He discerns the need, and clearly and faithfully reads what to us is only a groan or agony. Then with mighty intercession, with groanings which cannot be uttered, He brings those needs before God and prays us through.

Glory to God! Do you wonder that the Spirit prays through us? Since God gave me a revelation (in part, at least) of my heart, I am not surprised that the Holy Spirit was poured through me in groaning and intercession. O friends, let us praise the Holy Spirit for such gracious ministry. Isn't He precious?—the tender, undefiled, dove of God, the delicate, pure, sweet breath of God! How can He come into this deep? How can He move down into such unspeakable poverty and bring to the surface the need and pray it through? O friends, I do not know. The mystery of godliness is beyond us. But I *do* know He has come. Hallelujah! If we would yield to Him more He would do more praying and thus do a deeper cleansing.

What is it that issues from this deep? A cry. How long has the cry gone up? Since the beginning. For ages it has come from the broken, bleeding, sinning hearts of mankind, lost, undone, helpless, and needing God. Not only has it come up from the human breast, but *the whole creation groaneth and travaileth in pain together until now.* Up from this first deep mentioned comes an agonizing cry for God! God! God!! That is the greatest need in the world today. People think they need so many things—better national life, better politics, better social conditions, better schools, better homes, etc. This is only too true, but the deep need of man is *God*. The blindness of mankind is heart breaking. Too many are *playing* at life on the surface when they might be *living* with God where all these needs might be supplied in Him. Life without God is indeed a tragedy.

THE SECOND DEEP

Now a word as to the second *deep* mentioned in the text. As we found the first *deep* that of need in the human heart, so we find the second *deep the* corresponding supply in the great heart of God. It is the deep, mystical and sublime heart of Jehovah. Who knows its depth? The Psalmist tells us in Psalm 92:5, "*O Lord, how great are thy works; and thy thoughts are very deep.*"

Time or space do not permit us to trace or even suggest the unmeasurable depths of God's love. Even the first ingredient in the nature of God is quite beyond our understanding. The depths of wisdom veiled from the mind of man, the hidden counsels of His heart, the unsounded oceans of His grace, the deep places of His being, shrouded in mystery are only faintly dreamed of by mortal mind. Do you wonder that Paul wrote as he did? When a revelation of His grace came to him, he was overpowered and gazing, as it were, off upon the dim outlines of God's salvation and purposes for man, as he comes into the new creation, he cries, "*O the depths of the riches both of the wisdom and knowledge of God! how unsearchable are his judgments and his ways past finding out! For who hath known the mind of the Lord? Or who hath been His counsellor?*" (Rom. 11:33).

In Eph. 3:18 and 19 Paul tells of the nature of this second deep. "*May be able to comprehend with all saints what is the breadth, and length, and depth, and height; and to know the love of Christ, which passeth knowledge, that ye might be filled with all the fulness of God.*"

There is an accompanying hunger on the part of God that He might find expression for His love and an object upon which He might lavish it. We sometimes forget that God has an object in quest. In Deut. 32:9 we read, *"For the Lord's portion is His people."* This is a strange statement. Could not the God of the universe find satisfaction or delight with the angelic hosts? with some celestial order of beings? Could not the marvelous display of creative power in matchless order and grandeur fill His heart with satisfaction ? No, friends. We are humiliated to learn that the omnipotent God, Creator of the heavens and the earth, finds peculiar delight in the hearts of His people.

O, how wonderful are the ways of God! Can it be that in my little, cramped, uneventful life God should take pleasure? Yes, dear ones, if we are God's people, we are then His portion which He this very day is seeking. The deep of His heart is calling to the deep in ours. Hallelujah! I saw this afresh in reading the words of Christ, the bleeding Lamb, as He hung upon the cross in dying love, *I thirst.* How potent with meaning! So simple a word veiled unspeakable soul-thirst on the part of Jesus. I am sure the physical body was fever-worn, and pain-racked and from those parched lips came the cry, *I thirst.* But let us not read the surface meaning only. He voiced in such a strange and hidden way the real agony of His soul. Indeed He thirsted. But not alone for water, but O, infinitely more, that the full revelation of His life and death might come even to you and to me. It was the great heart of God *"in* Christ reconciling the world unto Himself."

We cannot help but ask, In the face *of this deep calleth unto deep,* is there no answer? O, friends, can you imagine a call going up from the deep of human need for ages, and then of the call going out continually from the heart of God and think there could be *no* answer? Thank God there is no such mockery in His plan. The marvelous scheme of salvation not only includes this strange call of *deep unto deep,* but it carries also the answer.

The deep of the human heart had not yet learned to call when God shaped that answer. He needed only to speak one word. In order that we as mortals might understand the language of God, when He spoke that word, *"it became flesh and dwelt among us"* (John 1:1, also 14).

The answer which God gives to the call from the deep in us is one word, *Jesus,* — That is enough. Is there a call today from some deep place in your fife? Let me tell you *again—Jesus* is the answer. There can be no need of spirit, soul or body but that one answer may be *given—Jesus, Jesus, Jesus.* Can we ever learn this lesson? Think not that God is ever going to speak another answer. *"For He spake, and it was done; He commanded, and it stood last"* (Psalm 33:9). This is the most costly and marvelous word God ever spoke. It is enough. As a thousand cries go up from our deep, we need only God's answer, Jesus.

Now just a word as to the waterspouts. Did you notice that the waterspouts are the occasion for the calling? A waterspout is a whirlwind out upon the water, raising great masses of it to considerable heights. How this speaks again of the work of the Holy Spirit. In Scripture He is spoken of under the symbols of wind and water. Here it is a strong figure—wind and water both in intense action. This is the mighty movement of the Holy Spirit upon the ocean of our fives. As the mass of water is whirled up into the air an immense vacuum is created. This seeks to be filled as in nature a vacuum always does. Thus we have a call. The *deep* becomes, as it were, vocal and begins to call to be filled. Has He not swept over your heart-life many a time in a spiritual cyclone and swept out great depths to be filled?

Praise God for the waterspouts! They are only the agents in the hands of an omnipotent God, destined not to destroy but to "make room." And as on the rolling sea the deeps are discovered by this strange phenomenon and the winds rush in to fill the vacuum, so will the Holy Ghost, like a mighty rushing wind, sweep into our troubled hearts and fill the vacancy and yawning deep. At the noise (call) of *Thy* waterspouts. Many times we think it is a cyclone sent by the devil; or we see the agents only. Thus when our vision is too local we miss the filling because we fail to recognize that the call is from one of His waterspouts.

So, dear ones, may we afresh yield to His working and not only let the call go up from our hearts (voiced, I trust, by the Spirit), but may we take courage in knowing the answer is waiting and will come back in comfort, rest, strength or grace as the *deep* in our natures may demand. Let us yield, that the surface and the shallowness may be displaced by God's waterspouts, creating within us such depths as shall receive the deep things of God. So doing, the sea of life is sure to be storm swept, not always smooth as the natural may desire; but let us remember He is Sovereign of the sea and that the life committed to Him is safe.

Outline for John Wright Follette's "Echoes of the Deep"

I. Introduction

   A. Psalm 42:7 as a prophecy of Christ's work of redemption

   B. The picture of a storm-swept ocean and a helpless soul

II. Alternate interpretations of the verse

   A. Deep calling unto deep as unknown depths of need moved by God

   B. The author's experience at the Grand Canyon and the significance of depth

III. The First Deep: The depths of the human heart

   A. The mysterious, hidden nature of the human heart

   B. The source of life's issues (Proverbs 4:23)

   C. The deceitful and desperately wicked character of the heart (Jeremiah 17:9)

IV. The inability of man to measure the depths of the heart

   A. The lack of correct estimation and honesty in self-examination

   B. God's ability to search and know the heart (1 Chronicles 28:9, Psalm 44:20-21, Psalm 139:1-2)

   C. David's prayer for God to search his heart (Psalm 139:23-24)

V. The dangers of self-searching and introspection

   A. The hidden things in the depths of the heart

   B. The need for God's grace and the life of Jesus

   C. The total depravity of the natural man

VI. The role of the Holy Spirit in searching the depths

   A. The Holy Spirit as the mighty Intercessor (Romans 8:27)

   B. The Holy Spirit's ministry of discernment and intercession

   C. The mystery and wonder of the Holy Spirit's work

VII. The cry issuing from the first deep

  A. The cry for God as the greatest need of mankind

  B. The blindness of people seeking other solutions

  C. The tragedy of life without God

VIII. The Second Deep: The depths of God's heart

  A. The unmeasurable depths of God's love, wisdom, and grace

  B. Paul's revelation of the depths of God (Romans 11:33, Ephesians 3:18-19)

  C. God's desire to express His love and find delight in His people (Deuteronomy 32:9)

IX. The answer to the call of deep unto deep

  A. Jesus as God's answer to the cry of the human heart

  B. The sufficiency of Jesus for every need of spirit, soul, and body

  C. The costliness and marvel of God's answer in Jesus

X. The role of the waterspouts

  A. The waterspouts as symbols of the Holy Spirit's work

  B. The creation of depths in the heart to be filled by God

  C. The need to recognize the waterspouts as God's agents

XI. Conclusion

  A. The call to yield to God's working through the waterspouts

  B. The assurance of God's answer to the depths of our need

  C. The safety of a life committed to God despite the storms

Here are 50 thought-provoking questions
for small groups or private study

1. What role does trouble play in our spiritual growth according to the text?

2. How should we view trouble - as an enemy or a servant? Why?

3. How can troubles make us either bitter or better? What is the difference?

4. Why is expecting justice in life not a biblical view according to the author?

5. How can injustice actually reveal our level of spirituality?

6. Why does increased closeness to Christ also increase sensitivity to hurts?

7. What are we seeking in our troubles - deliverance or development? Which should be first?

8. How did historical Christian figures like Paul demonstrate that spiritual greatness often emerges from troubles?

9. How does Joseph's statement about his troubles reveal a godly perspective we should emulate?

10. Why does the author warn against praying for exemption from troubles? What should we pray instead?

11. What role does the "I" (our ego) play in how we respond to troubles?

12. How can trouble become a "servant" to build character and release potential in us?

13. How is trouble described as a "threshing" process for saints to reveal finer spiritual grain?

14. What deep inner cry rises up from humanity's need according to the text?

15. How does nature itself echo this cry from humanity's deep inner need?

16. Why is trouble often the occasion where humanity cries out to meet God's answering cry?

17. What does the author say is the greatest inner need of all people?

18. Why does surface living neglect our deeper inner need?

19. Why can't humanity truly fathom its own deep inner need and cry for help?

20. How does God fully understand this deep inner cry even when we don't?

21. Should we attempt to fully sound the depths of our own depravity without God? Why or why not?

22. What is the ministry of the Holy Spirit in searching our deep inner need?

23. How does the Holy Spirit intercede for us according to God's will from inner groanings?

24. Why is yielding more to the Spirit vital for this deep inner work?

25. How does creation itself have a deep inner need and cry for redemption?

26. What composes God's answering deep to humanity's deep cry?

27. How unfathomable are God's depths of wisdom, grace, love and purposes?

28. What longs to fill God's depths toward humanity? Why is this so amazing?

29. What is God's special delight and portion according to Scripture?

30. How did Christ crying "I thirst" on the cross echo this? What did it really mean?

31. How is Christ God's full answer to humanity's cry?

32. Why is Christ enough to meet all our needs?

33. What role do the "water spouts" play in this calling between the depths?

34. How is the Holy Spirit the one who stirs up these water spouts?

35. Why do we often mistake the Spirit's waterspouts for attacks of the devil?

36. What vacuum do these water spouts create through upheaval?

37. How does this vacuum cry out to be filled by God Himself?

38. What does the author encourage us to do in response to these water spouts?

39. How can yielding to them create needed "room" for God's depths?

40. Why does the author caution about wanting smooth seas? What's missing there?

41. What is the safe harbor in the midst of the storms?

42. How can we know (from Rom. 8:28) that God controls the extent of the waterspouts?

43. What reserves of God come into our depths being revealed by these spouts?

44. How does the author's imagery of the ocean floor reveal untouched areas of our inner life?

45. What is the source of godly issues emerging in due time according to Scripture?

46. Why does yielding to this process require courage and vulnerability?

47. How does pride often submarine this process? What reveals this is occurring?

48. How does introspection often sabotage this deep inner work?

49. What assurance gives us boldness to yield fully to this waterspout work?

50. How does reluctance limit the fullness we could experience in God?

HATTIE HAMMOND:

A LIFE WHOLLY DEVOTED

I first heard of dear Sister Hattie when Wade Taylor would mention her so often in his messages. Few evangelists have left as indelible a mark on my life and ministry as Hattie Philletta Hammond. Her simple yet profound deeper life message, relentless passion for Christ, and uncompromising call to holiness have pierced my soul time and time again as I've listened to her powerful passionate sermons.

From a young age, Hattie lived and breathed for one purpose alone - to glorify her Savior and draw others into deeper devotion to Him. Whether preaching to thousands at camp meetings or to her own reflection as a child, her singular focus never wavered. That same intensity pulsates through every recorded message of hers that I have had the privilege to hear.

I can attest that even reading the titles of her sermons stirs something deep within my spirit. Phrases like "Drawing Nigh Unto God," "The Way of the Cross," and "Abandonment to the Holy Ghost" cause my heart to leap with holy expectation, knowing I will soon drink from the wellspring of anointing that flowed so freely through her life and ministry.

Without fail, as I listen, I experience a fresh baptism of the Holy Spirit's conviction, comfort, and commissioning. The deeper truths she expounds pierce through superficiality and spur me on to greater depths in my walk with Christ. Her words carry an undeniable weight of authority and unction, confirming that she lived in the very Manifest Presence she proclaimed.

In a world often enamored by hype and flash, Hattie's ministry serves as a pure and potent reminder that there is no substitute for unfeigned intimacy with Jesus and uncompromising obedience to His will. She modeled what it means to be truly crucified with Christ - a life so surrendered that His life flows unhindered.

I am eternally grateful for how the Lord has used this humble yielded vessel to deepen my walk with Him. Hattie Hammond carried the flame of Pentecost with integrity and impact, and I know I am not alone in testifying that its holy influence continues to burn brightly even now. May all who love Jesus be inspired to follow in her footsteps of full consecration to Him.

CHAPTER 3
YIELDING TO THE HOLY SPIRIT

By Hattie Hammond

GOD is tremendously interested in you and me. As members of His Church, we are the body of His Son whom He sent to redeem men and women from sin and to gather them unto Himself. "He shall see or the travail of His: soul, and be satisfied." It cost the Son of God such a price to create this great body of redeemed ones that today in His heart there is a deep longing that they should be all He has planned them to be. Today He is 'working in them, and one day He is going to be satisfied when He shall have gathered together a company of people who will do His full-will.

The Holy Spirit' has come into our lives to lead us into the center of God's will. He dwells in us and desires to talk to us about the Father and about the Son. No one knows the Father but the Son and him to whom the Son wills to reveal Him. How wonderful to have the Son will to reveal the Father to us! And how glorious just to sit in His presence while the Son is revealing the Father to us, talking to us and taking us with Him into His glories, riches, beauties, and all those things that the Son beholds in the Father!

Then the Holy Ghost will take the Son and reveal Him to us. He alone can make real to us the Lord Jesus, and teach us those things in Him that we could never understand. When the Holy Ghost takes the Son and reveals Him to us, how altogether lovely He becomes. Instead of finding it hard to sit in His presence and worship Him, we wonder why we do not tarry there more often.

It is wonderful to have all our inner being quickened and enlightened with a revelation of the Lord Jesus. We are made willing to yield to the Holy Spirit when we see what He has come' to do. Just yield to Him. Thus marvelous revelations will come to us through different' members of the body, as the Holy Ghost moves upon them.

God wants to teach us how to yield to the Holy Ghost, to acquaint us with the supernatural. We are altogether too carnal, too taken up with natural things. God wants to acquaint us with the supernatural, with heavenly things, with divine realities. He wants to teach us how to move in the supernatural. And as we yield to the Holy Ghost and be ministers the things of God to us through whomever He chooses and pleases, what glorious things we learn! We attend meetings to hear different speakers, but really there is just one Speaker. When others try to speak, instead of Him their words fall with' their own weight and nothing is accomplished. But when He speaks, using whatever vessel He desires, may God give us ears to hear.

The Lord opened Lydia's heart and she heard things. The Lord wants to open our hearts. He has many things to say to us. He has asked us to incline our ear to Him. There are things some have gone from one end of the country to the other to hear. They have thought what they needed would come through a certain personality, through : a certain evangelist. But it must come from the Holy Ghost, whatever channel He chooses to use. Listen to Him.

Jesus said, "The words that I speak unto you, they are spirit, and they are life." No matter what vessel He chooses to speak through, lie must do the speaking: His words minister spirit and life to us. If we receive His words all our death is turned to life; all our deadness suddenly disappears, and all our lifelessness simply goes. Our lethargy seems to drop off like a tattered garment, and we rise into His life with our whole being open to Him.

May God give us eyes to see Him. The Lord wants us to get our eyes off things, and see Him. When we do that, we shall see Him everywhere. We can see the Lord then in the most unlikely places and things. Things that seem homely and ugly in the natural, become beautiful. Have we been longing to see Him moving, to see His glory, to see His will? He has given us eyes. How precious when the Lord opens our eyes and we see. May our eyes be opened.

So many of God's dear children have veiled faces. Think of the wonderful days in which we are living, of this wonderful revelation of Jesus the Holy Ghost is giving us, this revelation of the Father, this coming together of the body of Christ, this calling out of the bride for the Lamb.

God is dealing with hearts, moving everywhere, bringing, the sheep in. He is moving by His Spirit; His power is at work in all those who will to see Him and will to obey and He is bringing each one in to his place in the body of Christ, getting ready for that glad day when we shall see Him and be with Him. May our faces be unveiled.

"When He shall appear, we shall be like Him, for we shall see Him as He is." We are going to be like Him. In the natural we cannot understand how He is going to work it out, but when we draw up close to Him, loving Him and trusting Him and continually yielding to Him, we know that He is working it out. In that day when we see Him and become like Him, we will just have to say, "Jesus, You did it all." That is the place to which He wants to bring us, where we really see Him doing it all. We shall be conscious of His acts, His, power, His interest in us, and His love over us. Oh, may He open our eyes!

The Word of God says that "out of the heart are the issues of life." From the heart come our thoughts, our desires, and our affections. The lips merely bring forth what is the heart. May He give us hearts to understand Him, hearts that are wholly given over to Him. Then out of our hearts will come forth spiritual things that will be spoken through our lips, and the Holy Ghost will cause us to say things we never heard before. The Lord can teach us a lot of things out of our own mouths when our hearts are given over entirely to Him and He is the Lord of our inner natures. He will bring forth those things that will feed the Church and meet the need of the saints. It will not be just a lot of idle words, not the curiosities of the day, not the things that merely satisfy the old self, but things that will bring to us a revelation of Christ, that will satisfy our hearts with Him.

And as we yield to Him He will be satisfied with us. He wants to put each of us in His proper place In the body He wants to, He is trying to, He is doing it. If we do not step into our place in the body of Christ, someone else will, so as He moves upon you, be quick to respond, quick to yield, quick to say, "Yes." In meekness and humility yield up all. Let Him have His way. Say to Him, "Speak, Lord, for Thy servant heareth." And as He speaks, yield. He will get His will done. He will do the things that we have been praying perhaps for years that He would do, if we just yield, wait, and trust. He will bring us into that place in Himself which will mean victory for us, for the world, and for Himself. Through His body, the Church, He must reach the world. He is preparing for that and He must do it quickly; may He help us to take our place.

Outline for Hattie Hammond's
"Yielding to the Holy Spirit"

I. Introduction

   A. God's interest in His people as the body of His Son

   B. The Son's desire to see the travail of His soul satisfied

II. The role of the Holy Spirit in the life of a believer

   A. Leading us into the center of God's will

   B. Revealing the Father and the Son to us

   C. Making the Lord Jesus real and lovely to us

III. The need to yield to the Holy Spirit

   A. Becoming acquainted with the supernatural and heavenly things

   B. Learning to move in the supernatural by yielding to the Holy Spirit

   C. Receiving revelation through various members of the body as the Holy Spirit moves

IV. The importance of listening to the Holy Spirit

   A. The Lord's desire to open our hearts and speak to us

   B. The life-giving power of Jesus' words spoken through the Holy Spirit

   C. Rising into His life with our whole being open to Him

V. Seeing the Lord and having our eyes opened

   A. Getting our eyes off things and seeing Him everywhere

   B. Seeing His glory, His will, and His movement

   C. The danger of having veiled faces and missing the wonderful days we are living in

VI. God's work in preparing the Church

   A. Dealing with hearts and bringing the sheep into the body of Christ

B. Preparing for the day when we shall see Him and be like Him

C. Recognizing that Jesus is doing it all as we yield to Him

VII. The importance of our hearts being wholly given over to God

A. The heart as the source of life's issues (thoughts, desires, and affections)

B. The Holy Spirit bringing forth spiritual things through our lips when our hearts are yielded

C. Feeding the Church and meeting the needs of the saints through a revelation of Christ

VIII. Finding our place in the body of Christ

A. God's desire to put each one in their proper place

B. The need to be quick to respond, yield, and say "Yes" to the Holy Spirit

C. Stepping into our place or risking someone else taking it

IX. The results of yielding to the Holy Spirit

A. Victory for ourselves, the world, and for God

B. Being brought into a place in God that we have been praying for

C. God reaching the world through His body, the Church

X. Conclusion

A. The urgency of God's preparation and the need to take our place quickly

B. A call to yield, wait, and trust in the Holy Spirit's leading.

Here are 15 thought-provoking questions for small groups or private study

1. What does it mean to you that God is "tremendously interested" in you? How might this change your perspective?

2. Why do you think allowing the Holy Spirit to reveal Jesus to us makes Him become "altogether lovely"?

3. What areas of your life do you need to yield more fully to the leading of the Holy Spirit? What is holding you back?

4. How can you become less "carnal" and more attuned to heavenly realities and the supernatural movement of God?

5. Do you actively listen for the Holy Spirit's voice and prompting when you gather with other believers? What gets in the way?

6. How can the body of Christ "reach the world" more effectively? What is your role?

7. What false things tend to capture your gaze and distract you from keeping your eyes on Jesus?

8. Do you believe God can "work out" you becoming like Jesus in the end? Why or why not?

9. What has God been speaking to you lately? Are you responding with obedience?

10. Who do you need to forgive or release resentment toward in order to be fully yielded to God?

11. What passions and desires need to be surrendered so your words align with God's heart?

12. How will you posture yourself to "hear things" from the Lord's opened hand?

13. Do you truly want to discover God's full will for your life? What would change if you did?

14. Are you actively placing yourself in a position for God to use you to build up others in the body of Christ?

15. How can you cultivate a deeper awareness of God's love for you this week?

How can I be holy?

By Hattie Hammond

Because it is written, Be ye holy, for I am holy (I Peter 1:16).

I want to be holy! Jesus wants me to be holy! Seven times in the book of Leviticus God says, **"Ye shall be holy, for I am holy."** Then Paul writes in I Thess. 4:7, **"God has called us to holiness"**, and in I Thess. 5:24, **"Faithful is He that calleth you, who also will do it."**

We have three marvelous examples of holiness. Holy is the Father; Holy is the Son; and Holy is the blessed Holy Spirit. The main work of the Holy Trinity in the earth today is to call out a people for Himself and make them holy, as He is holy. Luke 1:17, **"To make ready a people, prepared for the Lord."**

In His holy atonement on the cross of Calvary, Jesus has made every provision to bring this to pass. He made an atonement for our spirit, our soul, and our body, and that is all there is to any of us. You know God is a holy God, I Peter 1:16. He wants His people to be holy. Why? Because the living Head of the Church is holy and He will have a body, a Church that is holy. He will have a bride that is holy. He will not be unequally yoked with a worldly, fleshly, carnal, unholy bride but a bride that is holy as He is holy.

Holiness is the very nature and character of God. That is why all Heaven sings, **"Holy is He that Is, Holy is He that Was, Holy is He that Evermore Shall Be."** Rev. 4:8 and Rev. 20:6 says, **"Holy is He that has part in the first resurrection." "And you that were sometimes alienated and enemies in your mind by wicked works, yet now hath He reconciled in the body of His flesh through death, to present you holy and unblameable and unreproveable in His sight:"** (Col. 1:21, 22).

Oh wonderful Jesus! How we love and adore Him for so great a salvation!

Yes, we want to be holy, we must be holy, but how can we be holy when we know we are so unholy? My dear friends, if you will read this pamphlet (chapter) through to the end, I am sure you will find your answer. We have to begin where Jesus began.

I must talk to you about something you have heard but may not understand. Do you know what really happened to you when you were born again? Thousands do not know. You say, "My sins were forgiven." Yes, but that is an Old Testament experience. Nicodemus knew he could take a little lamb to the temple for a sin offering and have his sins forgiven, but all his works brought no impartation of divine life to him. One day, he met Jesus and felt He had the answer. So he went to him "by night." That is how all of us have come to Jesus since the fall—"by night." There was "night" in our spirit, our soul and our body.

So Jesus said, "Ye must be born again." This is more than sins forgiven, more than Church membership, more than taking Communion, more than water baptism. Jesus gave Nicodemus John 3:16: **"For God so loved the world that He gave His only begotten son, that whosoever believeth on Him should not perish, but have everlasting life."** Have something! Now have everlasting life—a quality of life in which is a new source of life: in which is the possibility of a whole new existence. This is the beginning of God in you.

I John 5:12 says, **"He that hath the Son, hath life."** Then I must have the Son to have everlasting life in me? Yes, the Son will come into you. St. John 14:23, Jesus said, **"The Father and I will come to you, and take up our abode with you."** II Cor 6:16, **"Ye are the temple of the living God,"** and God hath said, **"I will dwell in you."** God promises He will take up His residence in you, the abode He wants to control. II Cor. 6:16, **"I will dwell in them and walk in them. I will be their God and they shall be my people."**

He is our Mighty God, our "Everlasting Father." Isa. 9:6. He is our Father: He fathered us. If He has fathered us, then we have His holy nature, the very nature of God. God will come into us in the new birth.

This is the new creation, God in us—Jesus in us in a new creation, II Cor. 5:17, subduing the old flesh, crucifying the old nature, casting out the devil, overcoming the world, conquering all His enemies in us, until there is none of self but Christ is all and in all. Hallelujah! Christ is in you.

The new birth is the beginning of God in you. This is the secret of how you can be holy, as He is Holy. You have the Holy Christ in you. He is now your life, your new nature. The new you is Christ. The old 'you' is not you anymore. The Holy Christ lives in you, a life that has never been in you before; a power, a dynamic that has never been in you before. In that life is the very holiness of God. The very essence of God is imparted to you. II Cor. 5:17 says, **"Old things are passed away, behold all things have become new."** Say it over and over again, "The old you isn't you anymore." He is our "Everlasting Father"—He fathers us. Let's find that in the scriptures. Look at I Peter 1:23. **"Being born again, not of corruptible seed, but of incorruptible. By the word of God, which liveth and abideth forever."** Who is the Word of God? Jesus is the Word of God. John 1:1.

He directs our attention to a seed. He fathers this new creation that is "in you" and He talks to us about the seed. Now read on and you will find something precious. Maybe you are 20, 30, 50, 60 years of age, but the beginning of you was a teeny-weeny seed that you could hold by the hundreds on the end of your finger. Is that right? Yes, well, potentially, in that little seed was all that you are right now.

Your eyes were in that little seed. Your ears were in that little seed. Your heart, your brain, your lungs, every organ in your body, your hands, your feet were in that little seed. Your nature was in that little seed, and if you live to be a hundred years old, all you will ever need is in that seed. It just needs to be released, to evolve, to develop and mature. But this seed has no spiritual life in it. It's a corruptible seed, full of old Adam's poison, the work of the flesh. Gal.5:19–21, **"Adultery, fornication, uncleanness, lasciviousness, idolatry, witchcraft, hatred,**

variance, emulations, wrath, strife, seditions, heresies, envyings, murders, drunkenness, revelings and such like. They which do such things, shall not enter the kingdom of God."

We must be born again spiritually of an incorruptible seed (incorruptible means it has everlasting life in it, it will never die—just as Jesus said, "shall not perish, but have everlasting life").

Who is this incorruptible seed? He is introduced to us by God in that passage in Genesis, fittingly considered by many as the first Gospel, the first good news. God speaking to Satan says, Genesis 3:15, **"I will put enmity between thee and the woman, and between thy seed and her seed. It shall bruise thy head and thou shall bruise his heel."** Man, God's precious creation, sold under sin, hears from God the promise of a glorious deliverance and victory. His own seed, conceived by the Holy Spirit in the womb of Mary, would engage in a battle against Satan and Satan's seed—sin, sickness, death, hell, and the grave—and overcome him, accomplishing our deliverance. Faith-filled hearts receive the incorruptible seed, "the Word of God," which is His eternal truth, His righteousness, His pure nature, His love for the Heavenly Father, and that power **"by which He is able to subdue all things unto Himself."** Phil. 3:21. This is the power in us that enables us to be holy as He is holy.

This truth, this power, this love, this life is all in the incorruptible seed which God plants in our lives, in the new birth. In this seed is all the **"fruit of the spirit; Love, joy, and Peace, Longsuffering, Gentleness, Goodness, Faith, Meekness, and Temperance." (Gal. 5:22, 23) "Walk in the spirit and you shall not fulfill the lusts of the flesh."** (Gal. 5:16) These two forces within us are constantly fighting each other to win control and our wishes are never free from their pressure. These two natures are like Siamese twins, one must die so that the other can live. 1 John 3:9, **"Whosoever is born of God, doth not commit sin, for His seed remaineth in him."**

Holiness is a character quality. Holiness is not given to us as a gift. When we are born again, we receive Christ's nature, given to us as a gift, imparted to us on the basis of His redemption, but character qualities are the products of discipline; overcoming of trials, sorrow, heartaches, hardships, and intensive spiritual living. Christ is in us but only as we let Him live can holiness be lived out through us. Instead of anger, let His love live; instead of impatience, let the Patient One live His patience through us. "That which is born of the flesh is flesh. That which is born of the spirit is spirit." Even though we are born again, it is still possible to sow to the flesh. God in His mercy shows us the utter folly, the utter ruin, the utter futility, the utter vanity of the carnal realm. We must sow to the spirit. God, help us to realize that the more we live in the spirit the less will the world and the flesh, with its traps and snares that the enemy has set for our feet, be able to catch us. It is either - or; the flesh or the spirit, the carnal or the spiritual, the world, the flesh and the devil or the Holy, the pure, the heavenly.

Father, Son, and Holy Spirit are on our side. Jesus is coming for a Church, a people who believe the character of Jesus can be lived in His people. (Co. 2:6.) **"As ye have received Christ Jesus the Lord, so walk ye in Him."** To be in Christ Jesus means to be separated, emancipated, hidden, protected in Him, holy in all manner of conversation.

We hear folks say, "Why am I here? What is this life all about?" God has given us three score years and ten. Why? For the purpose, the privilege of receiving His incorruptible seed in preparation for the next life. This life is not the real thing. This is just the second phase (as it were). Three score years and ten to prepare for the real thing, the eternal ages with God, and potentially all that God will ever ask of us, all that God will ever require of us. All that we will ever be throughout the eternal ages, potentially, is in that incorruptible seed, which is, "Christ in you, the Hope of Glory."

We were nine months preparing for the Earth life, now He gives us three score years and ten to prepare for the eternal ages. There are three lives that we live; the first one is nine months long, in which we are making all of our preparations to live in this world. We are growing eyes and ears, hands and feet, and all the instruments we will need to live in this world, and then Paul says in I Cor. 13:10, **"When that which is perfect is come, that which is in part shall be done away."** So we discard the old house and we are born a perfect little human being.

We soon learn that we need those two feet to walk and aren't we glad we have two good eyes to see this beautiful spring God has given us and ears to hear the song of the birds and the laughter of little children? We are only given three score years and ten because this isn't the real thing. This life is not just to make money, to purchase things, and to add land to land, car to car, marry and raise children. The real purpose of this life, from God's point of view, is that we surrender our total being, spirit, soul, and body to Him; that we be born again spiritually; that we receive the incorruptible seed, His Holy Son, in us in which is the possibility of all our eternity with God, and from that seed He can reap the harvest He wants. The next life is the real life that we'll live with Him through eternal ages.

Have you ever planted seed? Only living seed will grow. When you plant corn, you want to reap corn. When you plant potatoes, you want to reap potatoes. When the Father plants His Holy Son in us, He wants to reap a full-grown Christ. Jesus becomes our new self. "I live, yet not I, but Christ liveth in me." The old you isn't you anymore. Jesus is the new you. Jesus is alive in you. Jesus in your new life. You are a new creation and everything that God wants waits to be released in you. Feed that new life. Something wonderful is happening inside of you. Is it real to you that Jesus lives in you? Is His life really your life? Then you can be holy with the holiness of God. You can be righteous with His righteousness because it is not you but Christ who liveth in you. Let Him stand up in you and meet your circumstances. Let Him live and reign through your trials and temptations. He is all you need to live a holy, victorious, overcoming life.

Thanks for reading until now, my dear, but please read on, this is the most important part.

When Jesus comes for us (and we are expecting Him so soon), only what His Holy Christ within us has developed will go. Only as much of Christ as we have "put on" (developed), only that will go into the rapture. This incorruptible seed is the new you, the new creation you. The new man in you is Christ. Feed that new life in you. Feed on His Word, live in the Spirit. Jesus said, "My meat and my drink is to do the will of Him that sent me." Do His will; eat His Word; stay in His presence.

Paul says in I Cor. 15:23, **In the resurrection, "every man in his own order"** (in his own cohort, or regiment, or for whatever we have qualified, so indeed we must be holy). We can be holy because the Holy Christ is now our life. His nature is our new nature. It wasn't hard to be like our parents, we had their nature. It isn't hard to be like Jesus. We have His Holy nature and in Him we see Him, so we shall be like Him for we shall see Him as He is.

While I was ministering in Indiana, a twelve-year-old boy asked us to pray for him. He said, "I am being persecuted. Today the persecutor was troubling me. I remembered what you said that Jesus was inside me. I should let Him meet my foes, my troubles and my trials, so I stood still and prayed, saying, 'Jesus, the devil is at the door, will you please answer the door for me?' And when the devil saw who was inside of me, he said, 'Excuse me, please. I'm at the wrong house.'"

When you plant seed, you want the rain to water it so it will grow. Jesus has promised the believer the "latter rain." It will come on the seed and cause it to grow. Joel 2:23, **"Not by might, nor by power, but by my Spirit sayeth the Lord."** Zech. 4:6.

The holy Seed, the Holy Christ is in you: the dynamic, the power to live a holy life, so put off the old man, Eph. 4:22; put on the new man and let Him live.

We must grow; we must mature, for when Jesus comes for us, only Jesus will go to be united with the Holy Son of God. **"He that is holy will have part in the first resurrection."**

Outline for Hattie Hammond's "How Can I Be Holy?"

I. Introduction

    A. God's call to holiness (I Peter 1:16, Leviticus, I Thess. 4:7)

    B. The Holy Trinity as examples of holiness

    C. Jesus' provision for holiness through His atonement

II. The necessity of holiness

    A. God's holy nature and character

    B. The requirement for a holy Church and bride

    C. The reconciliation through Christ to present us holy (Col. 1:21, 22)

III. The new birth and its implications

    A. The inadequacy of Old Testament experiences

    B. The meaning of being born again (John 3:16)

    C. Receiving everlasting life and a new source of life

    D. God dwelling in us as His temple (II Cor. 6:16)

IV. The incorruptible seed and the new creation

    A. The analogy of a natural seed and its potential

    B. The corruptible seed of Adam and its works (Gal. 5:19-21)

    C. The incorruptible seed, Christ, and His victory over Satan (Gen. 3:15)

    D. The fruit of the Spirit in the incorruptible seed (Gal. 5:22, 23)

V. The development of holiness as a character quality

    A. The gift of Christ's nature in the new birth

    B. The necessity of discipline and overcoming trials

    C. Letting Christ live through us in place of the flesh

VI. The purpose of this life

    A. The three phases of life: in the womb, on earth, and in eternity

B. The privilege of receiving the incorruptible seed in preparation for eternity

C. Surrendering our total being to God and allowing Him to reap a harvest

VII. The practical outworking of Christ's life in us

A. Feeding the new life through God's Word and presence

B. Doing God's will as our meat and drink

C. Qualifying for our place in the resurrection (I Cor. 15:23)

D. The ease of being like Christ with His nature in us

VIII. The power to live a holy life

A. The promise of the latter rain to cause growth (Joel 2:23, Zech. 4:6)

B. Putting off the old man and putting on the new (Eph. 4:22)

C. Letting Christ live through us and meet our challenges

IX. Conclusion

A. The necessity of growth and maturity for Christ's return

B. The promise of the first resurrection for those who are holy (Rev. 20:6)

Here are 25 thought-provoking study questions for small groups and private study

1. What scriptures does the author cite about being called to holiness?

2. How does the author describe the Holy Trinity's work in calling people to holiness?

3. What happened on the cross according to the passage that enables holiness?

4. Why does God want His people to be holy like Him, according to the author?

5. What does the author say is the key to understanding how we can be holy?

6. How does the author explain what happens in the new birth regarding Christ being in us?

7. What scriptures does the author share about God dwelling in us?

8. What does the author say our new nature is as believers?

9. How does the author explain the new creation in Christ using the analogy of a seed?

10. What does the author say is the difference between the natural seed versus the incorruptible seed?

11. Who does the author identify as the incorruptible seed according to Scripture?

12. How does the author explain that holiness is developed through discipline and overcoming?

13. What does the author encourage readers to do instead of acting in the flesh?

14. What does the author say is the purpose of our lifetime on earth?

15. How does the author explain the three phases of human life using time spans?

16. What does the author say will go with us when Jesus returns? Why?

17. What does the author encourage readers to do to feed the new life in Christ in them?

18. What example does the author give of a young boy overcoming persecution?

19. What does the author say about the promised latter rain and its purpose?

20. How does the author sum up the key to living a holy life?

21. What does the author say about growing and maturing in Christ?

22. What scripture does the author cite about those who are holy taking part in the first resurrection?

23. What is the author's central message about holiness based on Christ in us?

24. What tone does the author use in explaining these truths about holiness?

25. What practical encouragement does the author give for pursuing holiness?

Remembering Walter Beuttler: A Life Poured Out for His Friend Jesus

Walter Beuttler, born in Germany in 1904, immigrated to the United States in 1925. After graduating from Central Bible Institute in 1931, he served on the faculty at Eastern Bible Institute from 1939 to 1972. But his legacy extends far beyond the classroom. In 1951, during a campus revival, God called Beuttler to "go teach all nations," and for the next 22 years, he travelled the world, sharing the love and friendship of Jesus with all who would listen.

I first heard of dear Brother Beuttler when Wade Taylor would mention him so often in his messages. The more I learned about his life and ministry, the more I realized the profound impact he had on countless lives, including my own. Through his sermons and writings, I have been deeply affected, each time receiving a greater hunger for the manifest presence of God. It has been the honor of a lifetime to publish 3 of his books.

Walter's classroom was a place where the Lord often visited, revealing Himself and moving in the lives of the students. At the end of each visitation, he would smile and say, "Isn't He nice?" He encouraged his students to cultivate a personal, experiential knowledge of the Lord, using his own unique spiritual walk as an example.

One story that particularly resonates with me is when Walter was watching another pastor's church and the Lord told him to fast and pray. Despite initial discouragement, he persevered for seven days, believing that Jesus was worth pursuing. On the last night of his fast, Jesus appeared to him, speaking words that profoundly changed his life and ministry.

Walter's life was filled with remarkable adventures with his friend Jesus. Whether flying over the Atlantic, sitting beside the pyramids in Egypt, or ministering in the remotest islands, he lived in constant communion with the Lord. His stories weren't mere tales; they were living testimonies of a man who walked intimately with his Savior and was eager to share the depths of that relationship with hungry hearts around the globe.

Over his many years of ministry, Walter traveled to over 100 countries, logging more than half a million miles. He made ten trips around the world, crisscrossing continents and oceans to bring the richness of God's presence to people of all cultures. Wherever he went, the presence of God was electrifying because Walter personally knew and walked with the Lord as very few have.

I am deeply inspired by Walter's example of pressing in to know God more fully, refusing to take "no" for an answer. He showed us what it means to be desperate for more of God, to cry out from the depths of our hearts. This kind of earnest hunger and thirst moves the heart of the Father, causing Him to draw us into the inner chambers of His presence and share precious secrets reserved for those who diligently seek Him.

Walter Beuttler's life and ministry continue to impact generations, even decades after his passing in 1974. His legacy is one of a life poured out as a drink offering before the Lord, a fragrance of devotion that still inspires us to go deeper in our pursuit of Jesus. As his spiritual children, we have a rich inheritance in the example he set of unwavering obedience, thirst for God's presence, and delight in His friendship.

In a world often enamored by hype and shallowness, Walter's life calls us back to the simplicity and power of an utterly abandoned heart. He walked a path of deep intimacy with Christ, and his footprints beckon us to follow. Oh, that we would all learn to be such friends of God! May the fire that burned in Walter Beuttler's heart ignite our own, until one by one, we become that company of believers who seek the face of God with wholehearted devotion. This is the legacy I desire to carry forward.

CHAPTER 4
SHOW ME NOW THY WAY THAT I MAY KNOW THEE

By Walter Beuttler

In these evenings I expect to speak to you on the presence of God, and particularly what I would call the manifest presence of God. Thank God, God is pouring out His Spirit all over the world. It is amazing how many people, different denominations in the world, experience a fresh move of God. What I see here, and I see it every year as I go abroad, that God is giving to other denominations what many Pentecostal people have experienced, and I'm thinking particularly of the traditional Pentecostal folk. What many of them are turning their back on today, the other groups are receiving. It's a marvelous move of God, as you well know, throughout the world.

"And Moses said unto the Lord, See, thou sayest unto me, Bring up this people; and thou hast not let me know whom thou wilt send with me. Yet thou hast said, I know thee by name, and thou hast also found grace in my sight. Now therefore, I pray thee, if I have found grace in thy sight, shew me now thy way, that I may know thee, that I may find grace in thy sight; and consider that this nation is thy people. And he said, My presence shall go with thee, and I will give thee rest. And he said unto him, If thy presence go not with me, carry us not up hence." Exodus 33:12-15

I find this Moses to be a most remarkable man. I find the Book of Exodus to be a most remarkable book, particularly now with reference to the revelation of the ways and nature of God. This prayer of Moses, I have prayed many times. It is remarkable all the more when you consider the spiritual state of Moses at the time. For instance, we read in the very same chapter, verse 11, "*The Lord spake unto Moses face to face as a man speaketh unto his friend.*" Think of it! That simply means, at least to me, that God spoke to Moses, with Moses in fact, intimately as a man speaks unto his friend.

Now a friend will tell a friend what he does not tell everyone else. Friends very often have secrets between each other, and God spoke to Moses as a man speaks unto his friend. Think of it! And yet, notwithstanding that remarkable, intimate relationship of Moses to

God, he still prayed, *"Show me now thy way that I may know thee."* Why this man knew God already, but he wanted to know God still more.

One year I was giving a chapel message in school on seeking God, the need for seeking God, how to seek God, conditions for finding God, etc. One of the teachers challenged me and said, *"Brother Beuttler* (and he was quite critical), *Why do you tell these students to seek God when they have already found him?"*

I said, *"I'm not exhorting them to seek the Lord because they never found Him, but because they need to find Him some more."* There is no end to God's disclosure of Himself to our hearts.

You know there is a passage in II Chronicles 26:5 that says, *"And as long as he sought the Lord, God made him to prosper."* That's my motto, incidentally. *"As long as he sought the Lord, God made him to prosper."*

When you read through the chapter, you will find it says, God helped him; God helped him greatly; he was strengthened greatly; his name spread abroad; his name spread far abroad. The king became well known because of his success, and the secret of it was the fact that, *"As long as he sought the Lord, God made him to prosper."*

Now there's a warning in there: It says, *"As long as he sought."* There came a time when he no longer sought the Lord. His heart became filled with pride and he died a leper.

This Moses knew God, and yet he wanted to know God even more. The Lord knew Moses face to face. In Deuteronomy 34:10 we read, *"And there arose not a prophet since in Israel like unto Moses, whom the Lord knew face to face."* Think of it! God knew Moses face to face. God had a personal acquaintance with Moses, and Moses had a personal acquaintance with God. And yet this man said, *"Show me now thy way that I may know thee."*

In Numbers 12:8 there was a dispute. Miriam and Aaron had talked against Moses. They were criticizing him for the Ethiopian woman, which he married. Now I do not know whether Moses made a mistake or not, but I do know that it was none of the business of Miriam and Aaron.

Have you ever noticed there are people in this world (not here, I know that!) that mind everybody else's business but their own and forget theirs? (Not here, so don't get mad at me!) Miriam was one of them. They were two, what I would call butt-in-skies. They butted into other people's personal affairs, and the Lord heard it.

The Lord challenged those two, and then said of Moses, *"And the similitude of the Lord shall he behold."* Now that word similitude is variously translated such as, and the form of the Lord shall he behold; the likeness of the Lord shall he behold; the shape of the Lord shall he behold. Think of it! I do not want to go into that area as we'll get too far a- field, but the fact remains that the shape of the Lord (not the material shape, we know that), but the shape, the form of the Lord shall he behold. Yet this man who had such a relationship with God that God said, *"I'm going to let him see my form."* He couldn't see His face, but the rest he could see-His back, His hands. That he could see. Yet this man prayed, *"That I may know thee."*

You know what? A true personal knowledge of God begets a desire for still a greater knowledge of God. There is no end to this.

In Psalm 24, using a French translation that I discovered in France, *"And the intimate communion of the Lord"*...the idea being God will give His intimate communion to those who fear Him. Moses had intimate communion with the Lord, and yet he prayed, *"Show me now thy way."*

Notice there are two things here: 1) Show me now thy way, that is, the way you do things, why You do them, where You go, why You go, and 2) That I may know thee. He wanted to know God's ways. He wanted to know God. In answer to his prayer, God let this man into the secrets of the presence of God.

Speaking of the Lord's way: Do you ever watch the way the Lord works? You learn so much about God if you just watch the way He operates. I'll tell you something.

One year, Hattie Hammond and I had a convention in Washington. The church put us up in the Ambassador Hotel, so evenings after the last service we would go down to the coffee shop, have some poached eggs, English muffins and talk, talk past midnight.

One night she said, *"Brother Beuttler, I must tell you something."* And I never forgot it. She said that she was out in Springfield, the A/G headquarters as you know. There was a huge Ambassador's Rally. Because she's well known, they asked her to sit on the platform with the other dignitaries, satellites, galaxies-ministerial galaxies! She was sitting there and a young fellow from the Christ's Ambassadors was the speaker. She said there was a huge attendance, a number of thousand.

She said, *"You never heard as bad a harangue and nonsense as that young fellow preached that afternoon to that huge congregation. It was awful. All he did was tear the A/G into shreds. Nothing but criticism, he told his audience all that was wrong with the Assemblies of God."* (Rightly or wrongly, that's beside the point.) When he got done, the power of God fell on that audience. Hands went up and they were praising the Lord all over the place, and Hattie was dumbfounded.

She said, *"I was so dumbfounded I didn't know what to think."* So she said to God, *"God, how can You bless such a harangue as we had to listen to this afternoon? Now Brother Beuttler, I want to tell you something. The Lord answered me and said, 'I'm not blessing one word of all he said. I'm pouring the Spirit of rejoicing upon My people to help them forget everything he did say.'"* So God took His eraser and erased.

I never forgot that and I say, *"Beuttler, if the power ever falls when you get done preaching, there could be more than one reason!"* In fact, I was speaking in chapel at NBI one year-had a real anointing, and I said something I should have never said.

"Under the anointing?" you ask.

"Yes."

"How can that be?"

"Well, I don't know how, but I do know it be!" It can be, something gets in. There was the river with a dead cow floating down. How can that be? Well, I said something I should have never said. It was true all right, but there are a lot of things true that shouldn't be said. While I was saying it, I knew I was making a mistake. The anointing didn't leave, but this thing got in.

Your mind can be just as quick as a computer, and my computer went ahead. While I was talking and faster than I could say it, I thought the thing through while I was saying it. I questioned myself, *"Should I stop and correct it or what to do?"*

Quicker than lightening the thought went through my mind, *"No, half the students won't be listening anyway, so they won't get hurt; and for the rest, if I try to explain it, I only draw attention to it and then they will remember it."* So I went right ahead. That went like this, and I had the answer, if you know what I mean.

When I got done with my statement, we had a beautiful utterance in tongues and interpretation. It was exquisite! The students were shouting their ears off almost. I knew what happened. God used His eraser! That wasn't blessing the statement I had made, it was erasing it. God has wonderful, wonderful ways of working. *"Show me now thy way."*

Oh that we would (I say "we," I don't know you people, but I say "we" because I have to put it that way.) Oh that more of God's people would be more willing to learn the ways of the Spirit. You see because in our day we're in the intellectual trend that is gradually whittling away at the things of the Spirit of God – and don't you kid yourself! It's so.

We had visiting in school a John Wright Follett, and he preached for about 3 hours. You could listen to him all morning. The whole school had to stop for him, and it was worth it. When he got done, he had given us a tremendous feast. At the end of the feast there was a message in tongues (not lengthy at all) and an interpretation, very simple, so simple you could wonder, "*What for?*"

One of our lady teachers, a good teacher, but tended to be critical in the things of the Spirit, said within herself (she told us later), "*Why do we have to have a message in tongues after such a big feast, and then just a simple little truth that doesn't compare with what we just had?*"

And the Lord answered her, "*Because I have babies in this audience who didn't get one thing out of all he said. I have to take care of the babies, the children as well as the mature.*" So the Lord sent His milk bottle or some baby food, some Pabulum for a few babies there who couldn't get anything else out of anything that man said. But then the Lord sent them a little portion. Oh! "*Show me now thy way, that I may know thee.*"

We're dealing here with a man who already had a marvelous relationship with God. I envy Moses.

Now notice what God answered. It takes us back to Chapter 33. "*And He said, My presence shall go with thee, and I will give thee rest.*" Moses, at this juncture, appeared to have been troubled or disquieted in his spirit, apprehensive. He had to lead these people into the Promised Land. He knew they were a stubborn people to be sure. There were dangers in the way. There were vipers. There were scorpions. He knew he had a job on his hand. Apparently he wanted some kind of a helpmeet, a companion because he said, "*You did not let me know whom you will send with me.*"

And then God answered and said, "*My presence shall go with thee, and I will give thee rest.*" Here we have the presence of God as a companion. I could not tell you, I could find no words to tell you how I appreciate the companionship of the presence of God. The Lord gave this to me once, "*My presence shall go with thee, and I will give thee rest.*" I travel all over the world, every year to all areas, the remotest places I get to, almost always alone, but not alone. There is that presence!

One year I went to France and as always I pray something like this, *"Father, don't You let me go unless You go with me."* That's my standard prayer before I go. I do not want to go without His presence. And I was going to Idlewild (now JFK) in New York and stopped in New York City, walked down 5th Avenue to take the bus out to the airport. On the way down 5th Avenue, I said in my heart, *"Father, please don't let me go unless You go with me."* Right in here (pointing to stomach), words came.

You may think me funny, but you can think what you like. I got over that long ago. As far as I'm concerned, this is the area where the Spirit of God lives, where our spirit is, where the Spirit of God is felt. That is where I get things from God; that's where you get His leading. This is where you have the peace. Now God leads in other ways, but this is one of them.

And right in here (stomach area), there came these words, *"When you arrive, I will be waiting for you."* Um Yummy! Isn't that deliciousmous? Oh, Brother Beuttler, that's not in the dictionary. Well, I know that, but it's in mine. It's Beuttler's dictionary- deliciousmous. *"When you arrive, I will be waiting for you."* You see folkses, this thing is real. It gets realer all the time.

I arrived at Oley Airport next morning, and it was raining cats and dogs, pitchforks, sauerkraut, lima beans, succotash, everything came down. Oley Airport was just like a lake with heavy drops. It poured. I stepped off the plane; stepped on the concrete all covered with water, and folks, there was the enveloping presence, a strong sense of the Lord's presence all about.

He had been waiting for me. He didn't wait in the waiting room, He couldn't wait that long. He had to get out. And when I stepped on the concrete, there was the presence. Oh! To me those things are so deliciousmous, super deliciousmous!

Speaking of this companionship, to me, it's the life. It turns an airport into a cathedral, if you know what I mean. And I get to many of the world's airports and sit out many an hour, but oh how often that is a cathedral of worship, fellowship, communion, the garden of spices with my Beloved.

I was making up an itinerary, and I wait on the Lord and have a map on my desk of the world, not to find out how to get there (I know how to get there), but I look over it and want to get a confirmation in my spirit. So I was there and I was sure of the itinerary: Green Lane (Philly, of course), Los Angeles, Tokyo, Hong Kong, Manila, Singapore. After Singapore, I didn't know which way to go. I couldn't make up my mind.

I was sitting on the floor with the map on my bed. I put my hand on Singapore and said, *"Father, I know I could go down to Australia, to Perth, over to Melbourne, Sydney, come up through the South Pacific or what have you, with no problem."* Or I could go on westward, but I wanted to move in the Lord, you see. So I was sitting there for quite awhile.

Do you know what I mean when I speak of sitting before the Lord, waiting for the Lord like David? David sat before the Lord. That's where I get things; that's where you get things, not by running, but by sitting. I spend hours on a plane, trans-Pacific flight, hours sitting there waiting on the Lord: airports, hotel lobbies, what have you - love it. I sat there.

He heard what I said, *"Father, I just don't know which way to go."* And lo and behold, here it came, *"I will meet you at the Pyramids."* That was it. I knew what He meant, because in coming from the Far East to Europe, I used to like to come by way of Cairo, go out to the Pyramids. There's a hotel there, the Meina House, $3.oo/night, air conditioned, nothing sophisticated, very, very simple, nothing fancy, but clean and 5 minutes walk from the Pyramids.

So I knew what He meant by, *"I'll meet you at the Pyramids."* In other words, you go westward. That's what it meant to me. You know, you learn to understand what the Lord means. That comes with it. I knew what He meant - go westward. That tour meant India and what have you.

The day came when I was on an Air Indian flight to Cairo, and I had arranged to make about a three-day rest stop, sit in front of the Sphinx where there is a rest house. You can have coffee and Coke Cola.

You know Coke Cola is omnipresent, don't you? That's true. A thousand miles up the Amazon there's Coke Cola; the Arabian Desert, Coke Cola. They've got the secret. A challenge to Christianity, isn't it?

I was on the way to Cairo and very early in the morning (about 3:30 I would say), we were approaching the airport out in the desert. They were beginning to let down, and I was watching the lights of Cairo coming up at a distance, and I thought, "*I wonder where He's going to meet me.*"

I figured it would be down at the rest house. I'll go down there after I check in a hotel, have a cup of coffee, Coke Cola or something; sit there, watch the Sphinx, the Pyramids, wait on the Lord and while I sit there He'll be coming, but He didn't.

I was watching the lights of Cairo coming up when suddenly there was the Lord's presence, "*I will meet you at the Pyramids.*" He came out to meet me. Shall I put it this way, "*We rode in together.*" The nice enveloping presence of God. I hadn't expected it on the plane, but suddenly there was the awareness of His presence. "*My presence shall go with thee, and I will give thee rest.*" What a marvelous thing we have in this wondrous presence of God.

I was ministering on an island in the Far East, and we had a wonderful seminar with the national pastors - a wonderful week. The Spirit of God Himself even dismissed us at the end. The missionary that led the service said, "*Now let's stand and we'll dismiss this wonderful seminar.*" There was a message in tongues, interpretation, the Spirit of God Himself pronounced the dismissal. It was one of the most exquisite things.

And yet, there was a missionary there who had no use for me, or my type of ministry. You know, not everybody likes everybody. I'm not liked by everybody. Some preachers would rather give me rat poison than an offering to send me on my way. But that's all in the game. We all get that! The one missionary didn't care. He was in and out, in and out of the meetings, and I couldn't figure out what was wrong. Later on I learned that his wife ran away with another woman. She was a lesbian. No wonder I didn't go over!

Well, they took me to the airport, and my heart was down. Oh! I was down in spirit, because of these people's attitude. I stayed with them, but I had a companion. And I was walking out to the Indian Airlines plane to go up to Calcutta. I know my heart was down; I know my head was low. I was so depressed in my spirit. Usually I look around and wave goodbye. This time I didn't, but folkses, as I walked out to that plane, my cabin bag over my shoulder as always, all of a sudden, there was a word in here (stomach area), *"And the prophet Jeremiah went his way."*

I was thrilled. That doesn't mean God equated me with Jeremiah. God forbid! But what He meant was, *"Son or Beuttler* (I don't know how He thinks of me or what name He calls me-He never called me by name), *never mind."* Jeremiah went through the same opposition of his fellow prophets, and finally when he had no more to say, he went his way. *"And the prophet Jeremiah went his way."* That thing so strengthened me. To me, to this day, it has become a source of food when I meet with hostility, not often, but you meet with it. You go your way in the Lord. You have a companion, *"My presence shall go with thee."* I don't know what I'd do without it.

Quite a few years back I went to South America to Rio de Janeiro, then down to San Diego and over to Valparaiso, and my younger girl (and I'm very attached to my family) was small. Wife took me to the airport and she had Norma on her arm. I was sitting on a TWA Constellation (They didn't have jets then.) by the window and looked out. I saw that little girl weep; her whole body shook with weeping. She was on Mother's arm, her head was on Mother's shoulder and that girl just wept, that little body just shook. Well the plane started to move. I watched and could tell Wife was saying to Norma as she put her chin up, "*Look up, Daddy's leaving.*" And that little girl's body kept shaking; her little hand waved goodbye; her head turned aside; she didn't want to look. It was awful.

That thing went on the inside like a hot knife. I literally took hold of my chin and pulled my head over and said, "*Beuttler, don't look.*" I held my head there and kept it from looking until the plane turned and I couldn't see anymore. But you know, that thing stayed within me like a burning sword.

Down in Rio, I was up very early. The flight left at 5:00 a.m. The night before I changed clothes, shirt, what have you, had handkerchiefs, different pieces of clothing and there was a note: "*Dear Daddy, I love you very much. Come back soon.*" I put on a fresh pair of socks; there was a note, "*Dear Daddy, why do you leave your little girl? I'll be waiting for you.*" There must have been a dozen or so notes like that. Whenever I went for something, here was a little note. And it got to me.

Believe it or not, between Rio and Sao Paulo, I wept like a baby. I wept, I was so homesick, I didn't know what to do with myself. I looked out the window, watched the mountains so the hostess wouldn't come around and say, "*Dear sir, what seems to be the trouble? Can I help you? Will an aspirin do?*" I wept against the window so they wouldn't discover me.

In Sao Paulo there was a Pan American DC 7. I knew that flight left for New York and I almost panicked. I could have yelled, "*Get me my luggage, I'm going home.*" I said to myself, "*Beuttler, you're not going home boy. You just pull yourself together.*"

Well we left and got to San Diego tired (and I'm leading up to something). It was a long flight and a bad night. They put me on a choo choo train to Valparaiso. I thought they'd take me home and put me to bed and let me continue later. This was an all night ride.

There we went, chugga ta chugga ta chugga. I was so homesick and so tired. Later on I found out the missionaries didn't want to be bothered with a guest so they just sent me on to the others. You get that too. There I was.

Every day I ministered to a pretty large audience and inside there was a gnawing pain. If anybody knows what homesickness is, you know what I mean. I tried to snap out of it and couldn't find the snap. There was no snap. I literally looked in the mirror and said, *"Beuttler, I'm talking to you. You are not going home, fellow. You're going to Argentina, to Uruguay, to Paraguay, to Brazil, to Peru, and then in the fall, you'll go home, so snap out of it, pull yourself together."* Do you ever do that? I've done it more than once. This time it wouldn't work. I couldn't do it. I went to pieces with homesickness, for my girl especially.

That night I got out of bed and said, *"Father, this thing will never do. Either You do something for me, or let me go home."* And the Lord spoke, *"My presence shall go with thee, and I will give thee rest"* - the companionship of the presence of God.

I suppose you understand what I mean by this presence. I'm aware of God's omnipresence, but I'm not speaking of His omnipresence. I'm speaking of his, what I would call, His personalized or localized, His personal presence; an awareness of the sense of the presence of God. It's a marvelous thing with us wherever we are to be able to enjoy that marvelous touch of God's presence.

I'm not saying that I always have it, but it is, in general, a mode of life. I depend on it very, very much, especially in travel. So the presence of God here is a companion, God's response to Moses' prayer, *"Show me now thy way, that I may know thee."*

Now I'll take you to Psalm 31:19. This is also something that has been exceedingly precious to my own heart for many years:

"Oh, how great is thy goodness, which thou hast laid up for them that fear thee; which thou hast wrought for them that trust in thee before the sons of men; thou shalt keep them secretly in a pavilion from the strife of tongues." Psalm 31:19

Now surely in this town there never is any strife of tongues! But you get to some places where there is strife. I'm glad you agree with me. "*Thou shalt hide them in the secret of thy presence; thou shalt keep them secretly in a pavilion* (in a shelter, in a fortress) *from the strife of tongues.*"

Folkses, this presence of God, this awareness of that presence, that presence that makes you feel like saying, "*Praise the Lord! Oh God's real!*" I hope you understand. That becomes a shelter, a shelter in which, by which, we are shielded, saved or protected from the impact of the sharp words spoken by sharp tongues of hostile people. Any preacher knows how it feels to have the sharp tongue hit them like arrows, and they can get into your spirit and do an awful lot of damage. The presence of God becomes a shield.

This happened to me when I first started ministry in France. God had laid a message on my heart, but there were some refrigerators in the audience, especially among the leaders.

Then I said, "*Well Lord, if that's Your purpose, that's Your privilege. After all, You're God. I'll preach what You gave me come what may.*"

I started out and had a nice audience Sunday morning with a lady interpreter. Her husband was dead against me, against all Americans. There was a strong anti-American feeling in France at the time.

While I spoke, about 10 minutes, I felt in my spirit that somebody in the audience had the throbbing of the Spirit to give an utterance in tongues or prophecy. I didn't know which. I got it in here (pointing to stomach area). I could feel in here the Spirit of God trying to use somebody in the audience. Nothing happened, so I said to the lady, "*Will you tell this audience that someone has an utterance from the Spirit and should give it.*"

She said, "*Oh Brother Beuttler, we're not doing that in France. We never interrupt a speaker. The Holy Ghost doesn't interrupt Himself.*"

I said, "*Sister, this is not an interruption. This is partnership in the Holy Ghost. Will you tell them?*"

She said, "*Oh Brother Beuttler, we never do that in France.*"

I said, "*Will you tell them? We're going to do it now. How about it?*"

She grudgingly said, "*All right. The brother says, 'Somebody has an utterance from the Spirit and should give it.'*"

A lady stood up and gave a beautiful, powerful utterance in tongues and a man stood up and gave the interpretation. In the interpretation God bore witness to the fact that He had sent me to France. He bore witness to the word of God that had been spoken and asked the folk to accept the word, which He was sending in His Spirit. It went on...

Hands went up and shouting all over the place, and I heard some cracks in the refrigerators, "*Glory to God, Glory to God!*" I heard somebody down there and thought I knew the voice. There was the pastor, hands up, tears literally rolling down his face shouting, "*Glory to God! Boo hoo, boo hoo, Glory to God!*"

And that man came over, threw his arms around me and said, "*Brother Beuttler, God has sent you to France. We want you to stay as long as you can.*" He wept on my shoulder like a baby, and the other refrigerators and iceboxes behind him all melted and were as warm as could be.

Without exaggeration, as a result of that meeting, God opened up all of France to ministry and French North Africa. I've been there numerous times, and France has become one of my major fields.

This man who was so against me said one year, "*Brother Beuttler, wouldn't your family like to come with you sometime?*" I went back to be their national convention speaker for I don't know how many years. They had the family over also, sent us into Africa and paid all our fares. This man who was so hostile became the strongest Beuttler factor in France. That's how God turned him around, but in the crisis, had sustained me by the enveloping presence of God as a shield.

I was in France last summer. They asked again for this summer and the following year. I can go anytime I want. The field is wide open. They treat me and the family like a king. That's how God turned that man around. So much so, one year I was there and they said, *"Brother Beuttler, how about the convention next year?"*

I said, *"No, I'm going to Tokyo."*

They said, *"Couldn't you stop in France first? We'll adjust the date of the national convention to suit you."*

I said, *"No, I'm in school and will go straight to Tokyo."* He said, *"Well, pray about it."*

I thought, *"I have nothing to pray about. You can pray if you want."*

They had me in a hotel and that night the Lord awakened me again with his presence and a scripture, just a phrase, *"And they waited not for the counsel of the Lord."* I knew at once what the Lord meant. Do you see what I mean by the presence? It guides you and is with you; it speaks. That's how we move in God.

So I knew what He meant, *"You said 'No' to those brethren before you asked Me whether I wanted you to go back to France."*

So I said, *"Well Lord, it isn't practical. You don't go to Tokyo by way of Paris. It's too far around, takes too long."*

I wouldn't say now that the Lord spoke to me here, but I think He at least caused me to remember something. I knew there were flights from Paris to Tokyo over the North Pole to cut off that long route around India. It's a shorter cut, although expensive.

That came to me and I said, *"Lord, I suppose I could do it by going over the North Pole, but that isn't practical cost wise."* And I let it go at that, but I felt the Lord wanted me to go.

So the next day, the same man, who had formerly been so hostile, said, *"Brother Beuttler, did you pray?"*

I said, "*No, I didn't pray, but I got the answer anyway.*" He said, "*What's the answer?*"

I said, "*The Lord wants me to come, but I can't understand it. It isn't practical.*" He asked, "*Why isn't it practical?*"

I answered, "*There won't be time to go to Tokyo around India, and to go over the North Pole is too expensive.*"

My ticket was already over $2,000, and that's quite a bit. So he asked, "*How much is it going to cost?*" I didn't know but agreed to find out and meet him later on in France after I found out in Paris. So we arranged to meet in Marseille and he asked, "*Did you find out about the fare?*"

"*I found out all right, and it would cost an additional $500, which isn't practical,*" I answered.

He said, "*Brother Beuttler, if you're willing to speak at our convention, we're willing to give you the extra $500 to take you over the North Pole to Tokyo.*" That's what they did. And this was the man who was so hostile saying, "*I wish I had never let Beuttler into my church.*" He's one of our best friends to this day. The Spirit of God turned him around completely.

Coming back to Moses to kind of wind this thing up. "*Show me now thy way, that I may know thee,*" and God giving to this man this wonderful reply, "*My presence shall go with thee, and I will give thee rest.*" Friends, this manifest awareness of the presence of God is a wonderful companion going with us wherever we go. I owe this companion so much.

I was walking on the street of Tunis with my interpreter and had that nice little presence, the glow. Do you know what I mean by the glow? That glow of His presence. Mmmm! My! He's so real! It wasn't strong, but it was noticeable.

We walked along and all of a sudden this glow (very difficult to explain) turned into a very strong alarm. It's inadequate to explain but it's the only way I can put it. Such an alarm that it so alarmed me that I jumped to my right. I simply took a leap to my right without knowing why. I'm not as leapy today as I was then, but I took a leap, not knowing why.

As I did, a young Arab brushed my left shoulder with his right one, and he had a dagger, an open switchblade in his hand. From all appearance, he was ready to knife me from the back for whatever purpose, when my companion saw him and gave me the alarm of imminent danger, and I jumped away from his knife.

Those were the days when the Arabs cut the throats of the Frenchmen left and right. While I was in Algiers at that time, there was a busload of Frenchmen driven by an Arab driver over a bridge. The man turned the bus on the bridge, stopped crosswise. Two cars with Arabs followed in the back, got out and cut the throats of every Frenchmen in the bus. Those were the days when any Westerner was in great jeopardy.

From all appearances, this Arab tried to use his knife on me and my companion warned me. He tried a second time, but by that time we were alert and saw him approaching again. When he saw that, he went off. *"My presence shall go with thee"* as a companion and as a shelter to shield us from the venomous attack from all sorts of people that are stirred up for no reason or whatever reason. We have the presence of God as a shelter, as a shield to keep the arrows from penetrating into our soul and thereby destroy us.

"Show me now thy way, that I may know thee," is a good prayer.

Outline of Walter Beuttler's
"Show Me Now Thy Way That I May Know Thee":

Introduction:

- God is pouring out His Spirit all over the world in different denominations

- What traditional Pentecostals are turning their back on, other groups are receiving

I. Moses' Remarkable Relationship with God (Exodus 33:12-15)

    A. The Lord spoke to Moses face to face as a man speaks to his friend

    B. Moses beheld the form and similitude of the Lord

    C. Yet Moses still prayed, "Show me now thy way, that I may know thee"

        1. A true personal knowledge of God begets a desire for greater knowledge

        2. There is no end to God's disclosure of Himself to our hearts

II. God's Response to Moses' Prayer

    A. "My presence shall go with thee, and I will give thee rest" (v. 14)

        1. Moses was troubled and apprehensive about leading the people

        2. God offered His presence as a companion to Moses

    B. The companionship of God's presence

        1. Beuttler's experiences of God's manifest presence in his travels

            a) God's words: "When you arrive, I will be waiting for you"

            b) Meeting God's presence at the airport in France

        c) God directing his itinerary: "I will meet you at the Pyramids"

    2. God's presence strengthens in the face of opposition

        a) "And the prophet Jeremiah went his way"

        b) Beuttler's experience of hostility from a missionary

C. God's presence as a comfort in loneliness and homesickness

    1. Beuttler's story of leaving his daughter and battling homesickness

    2. God's word: "My presence shall go with thee, and I will give thee rest"

III. God's Presence as a Shelter (Psalm 31:19)

A. "Thou shalt keep them secretly in a pavilion from the strife of tongues"

B. God's presence shields from the impact of hostile words

C. Beuttler's experience preaching in France amidst anti-American sentiment

Conclusion:

- The presence of God is a marvelous thing we can enjoy wherever we are

- It is a mode of life that Beuttler depends on, especially in his travels

- God's presence becomes a shield and shelter from hostile tongues

Here are 25 thought-provoking study questions for small groups and private study

1. What is your biggest take away from this message?
2. How does a true personal knowledge of God beget a desire for greater knowledge of Him?
3. Is there a limit to God's disclosure of Himself to our hearts? Why or why not?
4. How can we cultivate a relationship with God where He speaks to us as a friend?
5. What does it mean to behold the form and similitude of the Lord?
6. Why do you think Moses still prayed to know God's way, despite his remarkable relationship with Him?
7. How can God's presence serve as a companion in our lives?
8. Share a time when you experienced God's manifest presence in your travels or daily life.
9. How can we learn to recognize and understand God's voice and leading?
10. Why is it important to wait on the Lord and seek His confirmation in our decisions?
11. How can God's presence strengthen us in the face of opposition or hostility?
12. What can we learn from the prophet Jeremiah's example of "going his way"?
13. How does loneliness or homesickness affect our spiritual lives, and how can God's presence comfort us during these times?
14. What steps can we take to cultivate a greater awareness of God's presence in our lives?
15. How can we find rest and peace in God's presence amidst life's troubles and uncertainties?
16. In what ways can God's presence serve as a shield or shelter from the "strife of tongues"?

17. How should we respond when faced with criticism or opposition because of our faith or ministry?
18. What role does waiting on the Lord and sitting in His presence play in our spiritual growth and discernment?
19. How can we maintain a sense of God's presence even in the midst of busy schedules and daily responsibilities?
20. What can we learn from Beuttler's example of vulnerability in sharing his personal struggles and experiences?
21. How does our relationship with family and loved ones impact our ministry and service to God?
22. What is the significance of God speaking to us through specific words, phrases, or scriptures?
23. How can we discern between God's voice and our own thoughts or desires?
24. In what ways can we encourage and support one another in seeking a deeper knowledge of God and His ways?
25. What practical steps can we take to make God's presence a consistent mode of life, as Beuttler described?

Seeley D. Kinne

SEELEY D. KINNE, THE MAN WHO LIVED THE DEEPER LIFE

Seeley D. Kinne was a remarkable man who rose from humble beginnings to achieve great success in ministry. Born in 1858 in rural New York state, he grew up the eldest of seven children helping on the family farm. Despite those humble beginnings, Kinne was driven and resourceful, and always sought to learn and improve. He eventually left his home to move to Avoca, where he lived with his wife and family for a time, boarding at the Gilbert residence on Church Street. He became an active member of the Pentecostal Assembly in Avoca, delivering well-attended sermons on a variety of deeper life topics at their weekly services. Throughout his life, Kinne was recognized as an outstanding minister who embodied the virtues of the deeper life and the bride. Today, he remains an inspiration to all those who encounter his story.

In November of 1932, Seeley was pastoring the Adullum Assembly in Rochester, New York when he wrote these powerful words that would go on to shape generations of believers around the world:

"Some regard us as fanatical. We are the clearest of excessive and disorderly workings that I have seen, so as to be free from bondages of almost every kind. True, we have dancing, singing, praising, and various spiritual exercises. To an onlooker that might seem boisterous; but to participate is to find the touch of God."

"Recently a blue cloud of glory has been seen in the upper part of the hall, which seems similar to the appearance at the dedication of the Tabernacle (in the Wilderness) and the Temple (of Solomon)."

"It is said that we do not have two meetings alike. There is always something new and fresh. Sometimes we have a meeting in which exhortation follows exhortation. On another occasion, prophetic utterances predominate. At other times, a meeting will be characterized by impressive testimonies, while on still another occasion, there is a mighty stream of prayer in the Spirit, which occupies the time wholly."

Seeley embodied a deep sense of faith and trust in God throughout his life, no matter how difficult or challenging the circumstances might be. This unwavering belief allowed him to accomplish tremendous feats and touch countless lives with his deeper message of the bride and divine intervention. Throughout his many years in ministry, he remained committed to serving others selflessly and spreading the deeper life message with every ounce of energy within him. His unwavering faith serves as an example for us all and inspires us to take every opportunity to follow in his footsteps.

Throughout his time in Rochester, Kinne continuously went above and beyond what was expected of him, always putting first the needs of those around him. He organized numerous community outreach programs and events and ensured that each person in the congregation felt loved and valued. And even when faced with difficult circumstances or over-whelming responsibilities, Kinne always strove to keep a positive attitude and maintain a sense of hope for the future.

Despite stepping down from his position as pastor in 1933, Kinne's legacy continued to live on through all those who were touched by his inspiring example. After leaving Rochester behind, he moved out west in 1944 where he lived in the home of his daughter for the last six years of his life. Kinne continued to make a difference in people's lives until his passing in 1950 at the age of 91. In dedicating so much of himself to helping others grow closer to God and experience lasting joy, Kinne made a powerful impact on all those whose paths crossed his, demonstrating once again just how powerful faith can be when combined with depth and compassion.

Seeley Kinne was a remarkable visionary who had an uncanny ability to see beyond his time and grasp a deeper revelation. He produced a wealth of insightful writings throughout his life, many of which still hold great value for readers today. By sharing these writings in our magazine **"The Deeper Life"** we hope to provide a fresh perspective on eternal truths and encourage others to seek a greater depth of understanding, beyond what is currently available. With his unique and distinctive writing style, Seeley Kinne was able to share his wisdom in a way that both inspired and motivated those who read his words. His legacy lives on, offering guidance and encouragement to those seeking deeper truth in an ever-changing world.

CHAPTER 5

A VISION FOR THE OVERCOMING CHURCH

By Seeley Kinne

1. The High Calling: Preparing for Christ's Millennial Reign

There is a common salvation. There is an earnest contending for the faith once delivered to the saints. There is a high calling in Christ Jesus.

In the majestic plan of Jesus Christ for the inauguration of His kingdom in its visible aspect, he has arranged for a selection of men and women, to have part in its conduct of affairs, who are suitable, and the manner of their selection is of deepest interest to us.

The Lord does the choosing, but there is a proper response to the Divine invitation, which is suitable for the called. The administration of the Millennial Kingdom will be entirely according to the will of Jesus Christ. He will be absolute monarch. But there is such a perfect balance between the love and mercy, and compassion of Jesus Christ, and the justice of God, that the sway of such an absolute monarch will be most delightful and attractive.

There will be no rebellion or insubordination among His assistants, for they will have been fully conquered, subdued, and so in love with Jesus the King, that to know His will and do it will be the universal delight of all.

Jesus has no selfishness in His nature. There will be no selfishness in the conduct of His Millennial Kingdom. Those who gain a place in those ranks will be only such as have been fully saved from selfishness.

The money kings with their gold, bonds and stocks, will have disappeared, along with all forms of greed and oppression. Two thirds of the population of the earth will have been swept away. Satan and his angels and every demon will have been banished.

The curse will be lifted, and thorns, weeds and thistles will no more infest the ground. Vegetation will grow luxuriant and the earth will bring forth bountifully. Deserts, barren and unfruitful places will become a garden. Polar ice will melt and the whole earth will become salubrious. Malarias, miasmas and diseases will abate.

The conduct of affairs will be by the Spirit, operating in prophecy, wisdom, and knowledge. Here and now is the place to be schooled and prepared. If you live on the earth plane now, you will not then be able to operate on the heavenly plane. Indeed if you are not thus prepared you will not be there.

Rule and control will be by the gifts of dominion, and government. Not by any such rude exercise of authority as men are wont to dominate and oppress in pride, pomp and severity. But there will go forth a holy, persuasive, invisible influence, the power of God that will be irresistible.

If you know nothing of these sacred powers, here, how would you be able to exercise them there?

2. Flowing with Rivers of Living Water

Contact the Lord and spend time with Him, and you will become like Him. The closer the contact, the more you partake of His nature. He is such a fountain of life that He imparts life to all who approach Him. This *"imparting"* power is resident in Jesus Christ.

"Draw near to God, and He will draw near to you...." James 4:8

"...When He shall appear (*draw nigh*)**, we shall be like Him; for we shall see Him as He is."** I John 3:2

There are varying degrees of fellowship and experience with God, as is taught by many Scriptural illustrations, such as the Outer Court, the Holy Place, and the Holy of Holies in the Tabernacle; the High Priest, the Priests, and the Levites in Israel; the three within the twelve disciples; the thirty-sixty-hundred fold.

"But in a great house there are not only vessels of gold and of silver, but also of wood and of earth; and some to honor, and some to dishonor." II Timothy 2:20

The kingdom of God is indeed a great house, in which are many vessels varying in quality, capacity, rank, and order. Our *"placement"* in His kingdom requires of us an extensive and particular course of preparation. A part of this is the development within us of a quality prophetic capacity.

"*Prophecy*" is the utterance of one who has developed this prophetic quality; one who partakes of God, of His Divine nature; eats the flesh and drinks the blood of Christ, the true bread of God.

True prophecy is God speaking by the mouth of man, yet it is more than that.

"...The words that I speak to you, they are spirit, and they are life." John 6:63

The prophetic word is *"spirit"* words, which are brought down to the human level to become words of life to the hearer.

"For the kingdom of God is not in word, but in power." I Corinthians 4:20

"And my speech and my preaching was not with enticing words of man's wisdom, but in demonstration of the Spirit and of power." I Corinthians 2:4

To merely speak the words of divine truth apart from an experiential knowledge of them is to be as a Pharisee, of whom Jesus said, "*They say and do not.*"" The Words of the Almighty are full of life and power. Christ has nothing in common with Pharisees.

For the Son of God to become the Savior of men, He first became the man Jesus Christ: a babe in a manger, a boy in the temple, a man from Nazareth who was a carpenter, baptized of John. He received witness of His Father from heaven through a voice saying, "*This is My beloved Son in whom I am well pleased,*" as the Holy Spirit, in the form of a dove, descended upon Him. One would suppose that His ministry would begin at once, but instead, "*Jesus was led by the Spirit into the wilderness, being forty days tempted of the devil.*"

Jesus must know the vicissitudes and sufferings of man with the various attacks, insinuations, and temptations of Satan, so malicious and painful.

"For we have not a high priest which cannot be touched with the feeling of our infirmities; but was in all points tempted like as we are, yet without sin." Hebrews 4:15

Not only did Christ personally meet and vanquish Satan, but He dwelt among the people. He met and shared their temptations, trials, problems, and sufferings. He ate with the publicans and sinners. He was too familiar with the common people to suit the religious leaders of that time. They had theories to promulgate, but He had spirit, life, and power to impart.

And He came to know, not by observation, but by experience, our afflictions and heartaches, that He might become a merciful and faithful high priest.

When Jesus spoke, it was the anointed prophetic word, gracious, full of spirit, life, and power. The dead came to life, lepers were cleansed, the lame leaped, the blind saw, and life sprang up wherever His Word came. For He not only spoke the Word, He had compassion. He felt, He knew, He experienced and lived in the life of the articulated Word. This is the mystery – that Jesus not only spoke the Word, He was the Word (John 1:1-5).

Jesus said, *"I proceeded forth and came from God"* (John 8:42). He proceeded as the living Word from the Father, and came forth into the world as a messenger sent by the Father.

This procession of the Word, from the Father through the Son, is a most profound mystery; and can be rightly understood only as God reveals it. That same infinite power that is in God, the Almighty Father, and in Christ, the Almighty Son, is in their spoken proceeding Word. Nothing of it can fail.

"Forever, O Lord, Your Word is settled in heaven." Psalms 119:89

And so of Jesus, the God-man, not only does the fullness of the Godhead dwell bodily in Him, but the fullness of man also. Jesus not only knew us by observation and discernment, but He participated in our thoughts and feelings, partook of our human (un-fallen) nature, and became a sharer in our joys and sorrows, our pleasures and pains, and all our vicissitudes: a merciful and faithful high priest, in all points tempted and tried, yet without sin.

We then are to become His ministers and share the eternal Word in its being spoken forth. This procession or coming forth of the Word does not end with the Son; but the *"Word of God was preached of Paul,"* the early Church, and onward through us (Acts 17:13, 19:20).

He who proclaims the Word of God must first partake thereof himself; he must eat the book – *"The husbandman must first be partaker of the fruit."* He cannot speak the Word mechanically as a mere machine, like Balaam's dumb ass. He first shall enter into its fellowship, and experience its meaning and life. This is a living essential truth, which lies at the foundation of the prophetic Word of God. It cannot be evaded without our becoming pharisaical.

"Let the Word of Christ dwell in you richly in all wisdom...." Colossians 3:16

"In the last day, that great day of the feast, Jesus stood and cried, saying, If any man thirst, let him come to Me, and drink. He that believes on Me, as the Scripture has said, out of his belly shall flow rivers of living water." John 7:37-38

To become a *"co-worker"* with the Lord in dispensing the quickened, anointed Word of God is a most exalted ministry. But it requires being a partaker of the Word before one can become a dispenser thereof.

Natural water carries, in solution, the elements of food. The water-of-life is the Spirit of Christ carrying the Word of God, His words and gifts. One who is prophetic becomes a dispenser of this living Word, and its miracle effects.

3. Awake, O Sleeper: Heeding Christ's Call to Spiritual Maturity

In each dispensation, according to revelation as then given, the Lord provided a way to attain perfection. Also, there were "representative" men who were examples of what the Lord required.

"Enoch walked with God...." Genesis 5:22

"...Noah was a just man and perfect in his generations, and Noah walked with God." Genesis 6:9

"...The Lord appeared to Abram, and said to him, I am the Almighty God; walk before Me, and be you perfect." Genesis 17:1

"There was a man in the land of Uz, whose name was Job; and that man was perfect and upright, and one that feared God, and eschewed evil." Job 1:1

The Scriptures show that Jesus required perfection (*growth into spiritual maturity*).

"Be you therefore perfect, even as your Father which is in heaven is perfect." Matthew 5:48

The word *"perfect"* refers to our being spiritually mature. Paul also testified to this, and to the faithful assistance that God will render to all who seek to fulfill His will.

"And the very God of peace sanctify you wholly...." I Thessalonians 5:23

Experiential blessings gained in one dispensation move into the following age, where they are enlarged and enjoyed. For example, Abraham became the father of all those who are *"justified by faith"* (Romans 4:8-16). The patriarchal period required a perfect walk with God. The dispensation of Law required the same, with additional ceremonial and moral obedience and sanctity. The Spirit dispensation requires a higher sanctity, along with an obedience to the leadings and workings of the Holy Spirit.

We are living in the *"time of restoration"* (Ephesians 1:10-11). Our privileges of experience are the highest ever known, since the attainments of the past increase, in the present. Healing, health, holiness, a walk with God, and a life in the Spirit are ours, bequeathed to us by past dispensational grants. All these are by way of restoration, and are given to us in a higher degree than formerly. And yet other *"new"* dispensational privileges, are being added as our inheritance in Christ.

Jesus Christ is taking <u>from among</u> the Church a *"Bride"* to Himself. This is a great condescension. For the Christ to take upon Himself the nature and form of man was certainly very humbling. But to take a Bride company from among men and then live through eternity with this Bride, in close association and fellowship, is beyond the comprehension of finite creatures.

A common teaching is that all classes of believers, regardless of their lack in attainment, will be part of the *"Bride of Christ."* His Kingdom is altogether different and apart from the earth realm in which man is found. How entirely unreasonable then, to suppose that Jesus Christ would consider and accept as His Bride, immature Christians, who have never sighted, entered, or operated in this higher spiritual plane. The conduct of affairs in His Kingdom will be on this high Spirit plane.

We cannot sow in the realm of the natural and reap in the realm of the Spiritual. *"Like begets like"* is an inherent law. *"Do men gather grapes of thorns, or figs of thistles?"* (Matthew 7:16)

"Let us rejoice and be glad and give the glory to Him, for the marriage of the Lamb has come and His bride has made herself ready. And it was given to her to clothe herself in fine linen, bright and clean; for the fine linen is the righteous acts of the saints. And he said to me, "Write, 'Blessed are those who are invited to the marriage supper of the Lamb. And he said to me, These are true words of God." Revelation 19:7-9 NAS

"His bride has made herself ready." The Lord is seeking out and qualifying a Bride. A clear vision and a practical understanding of the state and experience which is the divine standard for this calling is essential, if one is to enter this high calling. We must know and attain to God's requirements.

In past ages, in order to prepare a bride as a queen for her intended King, there were elaborate, prolonged schooling and various preparations that were required of her. Such an occasion is recited in Esther 2:8-13. See further Psalm 45:13-14.

Insight into the character and nature of Jesus Christ will help us to understand the characteristics He expects to find within His Bride. Certainly He will require her to be of like character with Himself. This speaks of our becoming an overcomer, by which we rise up into a state of union with Him, fully prepared to become His Bride.

"...Learn of Me, for I am meek and lowly in heart: and you shall find rest to your souls." Matthew 11:29

The rest of God that is described in Hebrews 4:1-10 is the result of our having ceased from all independent, self-activity. Jesus lived in this state of rest from the works of man. It was this perfect state of union with His Father which enabled Him to say:

"...Verily, verily, I say to you, The Son can do nothing of Himself, but what He sees the Father do: for what things soever He does, these also does the Son likewise." John 5:19

"When you have lifted up the Son of man, then shall you know that I am He, and that I do nothing of Myself; but as My Father has taught Me, I speak these things. And He that sent Me is with Me: the Father has not left Me alone; for I do always those things that please Him." John 8:28-29

"Believe you not that I am in the Father, and the Father in Me? the words that I speak to you I speak not of Myself: but the Father that dwells in Me, He does the works. Believe Me that I am in the Father, and the Father in Me: or else believe Me for the very works' sake." John 14:10-11

The Father's indwelling of the Son was the foundation of their union. Jesus prayed that His disciples also should be brought into this oneness.

"As You have sent Me into the world, even so have I also sent them into the world... That they all may be one; as You, Father, are in Me, and I in You, that they also may be one in Us: that the world may believe that You have sent Me." John 17:18, 21

The Father and Son, by the Holy Spirit, seeks complete control of the whole man, physical, soul, and spirit. Nothing less than a union such as this *"divine indwelling"* and *"co-working"* could satisfy God. This alone will constitute an acceptable Bride for Christ.

"Treat one another with the same spirit as you experience in Christ Jesus. Though He was divine by nature, He did not set store upon equality with God, but emptied Himself by taking the nature of a servant: born in human guise and appearing in human form, He humbly stooped in His obedience even to die, and to die on the cross." Philippians 2:1-8 Moffatt

If He, the *"Worthy One,"* so deeply humbled Himself, how lowly a place is our due?

Jesus humbled Himself and allowed those who accused Him as a blasphemer to spit on Him, smite Him, scourge Him, and crown Him with thorns. He allowed them to falsely bow as they decked Him with royal robes, and to nail Him to the cross between criminals. Although holy and undefiled, He took the defenseless attitude of a lamb, and became the victim for our sins.

The whole attitude of Jesus was entirely unselfish. *"The Son of man came not to be ministered to, but to minister."* He never did a selfish act. Never were the works of the flesh manifested in His life. Let no one imagine that an intimate association with Christ is possible without being saved to the uttermost.

"...These are they which follow the Lamb wherever He goes. These were redeemed from among men, being the first-fruits to God and to the Lamb. And in their mouth was found no guile, for they are without fault before the Throne of God." Revelation 14:4

"To him that overcomes will I grant to sit with Me in My Throne...." Revelation 3:21

To "*overcome*" means to experience victory, to master. The absence of a qualifying or modifying word means that we are to overcome in all ways, and in everything.

"Now thanks be to God, which always causes us to triumph in Christ...." 2 Corinthians 2:14

This complete overcoming describes the way to a seat with Christ in His Throne. Therefore, it is important to have a clear understanding of what it is to overcome, and the means and methods by which it is accomplished. Chapters two and three of the book of Revelation describe several phases of overcoming. The Church at Ephesus was commended, but with one serious reproof:

"...You have left your first love. Remember therefore from where you are fallen, and repent, and do the first works...." Revelation 2:4 -5

A return to their first love and first works was their only means of overcoming. Today, there are those who make a great showing outwardly, but have lost their original passionate love for Jesus, and the control of the Holy Spirit over their lives. If in any way, we are among these, return and restoration must be our first step, if we are to become overcomers.

The Churches at Smyrna, Pergamos, and Thyatira, also had much for which to be commended, but the Lord saw that there was among them the doctrines of Balaam, Jezebel, and Nicolaitanism. It is vain to think of being overcomers while linked with these false doctrines. Notice that Jesus is speaking in Revelation 2:24, to those who have not known the depths of Satan. They are admonished to "*hold fast*" and a promise is given them.

"And he that overcomes, and keeps My works to the end, to him will I give power over the nations." Revelation 2:26

In the Church at Sardis were those who were due for judgment. Their names would be blotted out (*Revelation 3:5*). If the Church at Philadelphia held out, they would receive the crown. Verse 12 speaks of the Bride of Christ.

The Laodicean Church which was rich and in need of nothing, in their own eyes, was *"wretched, blind, miserable and naked"* in the Lord's estimation. They were spiritually blind and needed heaven's eye salve, the Spirit of revelation. They thought earthly treasure was great riches, but of the *"gold of faith,"* the coin of the heavenly kingdom, they possessed little. To be spiritually naked, while outwardly clad in satin is a terrible deception. The Lord told them to buy of Him white raiment which speaks of spiritual garments.

It was this high estimate of their condition which caused them to settle into a self-satisfied carnal sleep. They became lukewarm which is to the Lord, a sickening condition. Many who are busy with valid responsibilities are spiritually lukewarm and lacking in godliness.

If we do not heed His warning to buy of Jesus *"gold tried in the fire,"* we too will be found of Him with only a pile of good works. That which appears to be gold to us may be only a stack of straw to be burned. Although straw and gold are the same color, gold is purified through refining fires, whereas straw is consumed.

In order to become His Bride, we must awake and overcome lest we find ourselves to have fallen short of His calling.

4. The Refiner's Fire: Entering God's School of Preparation

Those who aspire to be a partaker with the Lord in His end-time purposes must enter the School of Christ and be recreated, developed, and trained. These must pass through a process of crucifixion, testing, chastening, and correction.

The first thing necessary is to discover this School of Preparation, then seek to gain entrance. One must know that this course of training is available before he can enter its classes. A knowledge of its requirements is helpful; accepting them is essential. Unless we submit to this time of processing, our participation in His end-time purposes cannot be obtained.

Except we, in some measure, come to understand God's ways of working, we may find ourselves involved in that which is at cross-purposes with Him. He may be trying to crucify us through a certain individual, but all we see is someone trying to do us wrong. God may be applying the chastening rod, but we interpret it as someone wrongly abusing us.

If we can recognize God at work refining us, we will find ourselves in His School of Preparation, without our being aware that we have entered the process of our preparation.

Before we will be able to rightly relate to the classroom lessons of this school, we must come into a practical relationship with the Holy Spirit as our director and teacher. Each individual will be in a class by himself, and receive the lessons specifically fitted to the crucifixion of his will, heart, and carnal nature. These deal inwardly, backward in correction concerning incidents of the past, and forward in preparation toward the intended position and work to occupy us in *"that day."*

Jesus, the Master Rebuilder, is at hand, diligently working with fullers soap, refiners fire, winnowing fan, trying circumstances, and unreasonable people. He will bring to bear all these, and many other crucifying, chastening, and correcting people and trying things, which are exactly suited to our individual processing.

The only safe way is to face them all as being a test, in which we are to overcome. See no man. Rather, see it as being appointed of the Lord. The Lord will formulate conditions, and set in our path persons adapted to reach and correct our every crooked, or warped tendency. We must accept and understand the fact that it is the Lord at work.

An almost endless variety of incidents, and people, may gather about us. If we will remain steadfast and faithful, after we come through it all, we will have become a greatly changed person, and have become "...*a vessel unto honor, sanctified, and meet for the Masters use, and prepared unto every good work."* II Timothy 2:21

There are many who talk about end-time truth, but few seem to find the door that leads into this School of Preparation. Jesus said of the Pharisees, *"They say, and do not."*

"But be you doers of the Word and not hearers only, deceiving your own selves." James 1:22

"Let us rejoice and be glad and give the glory to Him, for the marriage of the Lamb has come and His bride has made herself ready. It was given to her to clothe herself in fine linen, bright and clean; for the fine linen is the righteous acts of the saints." Revelation 19:7-8 NAS

5. The Divine Process: Producing Overcomers

There is to be a practical application of the principles of overcoming, in our daily life experience. Wrought out by the working of the power God, overcoming begins with the recreation of our character.

Man, in his natural state, has within him a variety of ups and downs, extremes, and weaknesses of character. For those who are redeemed, and have fully committed their lives to the Lord, these tendencies must be dealt with. Only then can we abide in the anointing and power of God, and become a vessel sanctified and meet for Divine use.

These character variations occur in every part of the human makeup. No faculty of man seems so warped from its proper action, as is his will, especially in its proper attitude toward God. This has been one of Satan's master strokes. The basis of this satanic attack is to make it appear that the Lord's requirements are unreasonable, and that He is a tyrant.

Any fair minded person can be satisfied through a candid examination of the facts of individual and national history that God is truly benevolent, and has the welfare of man at heart. Rather, Satan himself is the awful tyrant and enemy of all good.

At the very heart of the Divine method of producing *"overcomers"* is the cross. To the unenlightened, the cross may seem cruel, but to those who are the called, it is the wisdom and power of God.

"But God forbid that I should glory, save in the cross of our Lord Jesus Christ, by whom the world is crucified to me, and I to the world." Galatians 6:14

"And they overcame him by the blood of the Lamb, and by the word of their testimony; and they loved not their lives to the death." Revelation 12:11

"By the blood of the Lamb" means that we are to rely on no merit of our own, but only in the perfect sacrifice of Jesus Christ. Because Jesus totally overcame Satan in our behalf, our triumph is complete. This puts us in an attitude before the accuser that leaves him nothing to charge against.

There are two planes, or realms in which the redeemed may live. The first is the carnal, flesh realm. The second is the heavenly, Spirit realm. Since we were born into the natural earth plane, our tendencies are toward that plane. A great transformation is necessary if we are to live and operate on the Spirit plane. The name of this process is *"crucifixion."*

This crucifixion is a death and burial process, as described in Romans, chapter 6, which is the destruction of sin. There is also to be a facing of the cross of Christ in our daily walk. Herein is the *"process"* by which the Lord recreates our character, which frees us from the natural realm, and lifts us into the Spirit realm. In these processes, He frees us from our strengths and weaknesses, the spots and blemishes of our nature, and gives us a heavenly character.

If we desire to become an *"overcomer,"* becoming a part of the Bride of Christ, we must enter the school of the Holy Spirit and come under His teachings, dealings, and control. Here, under the light of the Holy Spirit, we will face ourselves in thorough examination. No one can see in any other way his faults and earthward tendencies. With fan, refiner's fire, fuller's soap, chastening, these are the Lord's methods in dealing with these.

"But who may abide the day of His coming? and who shall stand when He appears? for He is like a refiner's fire, and like fullers' soap: And He shall sit as a refiner and purifier of silver...." Malachi 3:2-3

"Whose fan is in His hand, and he will thoroughly purge His floor, and gather His wheat into the garner; but He will burn up the chaff with unquenchable fire." Matthew 3:12

"...My son, despise not you the chastening of the Lord, nor faint when you are rebuked of Him: For whom the Lord loves He chastens, and scourges every son whom He receives." Hebrews 12:5-6

There is need of these crucifying processes in each of our lives. When we see our need, we should earnestly present ourselves to the Lord, to be entered as being His disciple, in *"The School of Christ,"* of which the Holy Spirit is Principal and Teacher.

If we are careful to listen, the Holy Spirit will show us how to apply the cross to all carnal tendencies, going deeper and deeper, until one after another, they are eliminated. At first it will be painful and hard to bear, but if we persevere, we will begin to glory in the cross.

All our carnal attitudes and ways will be transformed into the attitudes of Jesus Christ, and we will experience the great joy and delight of living untrammeled in the Spirit realm. Our liberty and attainment will be boundless, as all barriers are swept away.

Then, along with the Apostle Paul, we will be able to testify:

"I am crucified with Christ: nevertheless I live; yet not I, but Christ lives in me: and the life which I now live in the flesh I live by the faith of the Son of God, who loved me, and gave Himself for me." Galatians 2:20

Outline of Seeley Kinne's
"A Vision for the Overcoming Church"

Introduction: There is a common salvation, an earnest contending for the faith, and a high calling in Christ Jesus.

I.   The High Calling: Preparing for Christ's Millennial Reign

    A. God's selection process for those who will have a part in His kingdom

        1. The Lord does the choosing, but there is a proper response from the called

        2. The administration will be according to the will of Jesus Christ

    B. Characteristics of those who will be chosen

        1. Fully conquered, subdued, and in love with Jesus

        2. No rebellion, insubordination or selfishness

    C. Changes in the Millennial Kingdom

        1. No more oppression, greed or curse

        2. Conduct of affairs will be by the Spirit (prophecy, wisdom, knowledge)

        3. Rule and control by the gifts of dominion and government

II. Flowing with Rivers of Living Water

  A. Becoming like Jesus through contact and time spent with Him

      1. Varying degrees of fellowship and experience with God

      2. Developing a prophetic capacity

  B. True prophecy: God speaking by the mouth of man

      1. Words that are spirit and life, not just enticing words

2. Demonstration of the Spirit and power

C. Jesus' example of becoming a dispenser of the living Word

   1. Experiencing the vicissitudes and sufferings of man

   2. Becoming a merciful and faithful high priest

   3. The Word proceeding from the Father through the Son, and onward through us

III. Awake, O Sleeper: Heeding Christ's Call to Spiritual Maturity

A. God's requirement for perfection (spiritual maturity) in each dispensation

   1. Examples of representative men: Enoch, Noah, Abraham, Job

   2. Jesus' and Paul's call to perfection

B. Privileges and experiences increasing with each dispensation

   1. The time of restoration - highest privileges ever known

   2. New dispensational privileges being added

C. The Bride of Christ

   1. A great condescension for Christ to take a Bride from among men

   2. The Bride must operate on the high Spirit plane of His Kingdom

   3. Making herself ready through righteous acts

IV. The Refiner's Fire: Entering God's School of Preparation

A. The necessity of being recreated, developed and trained

   1. A process of crucifixion, testing, chastening and correction

   2. Discovering and entering the School of Preparation

B. The Holy Spirit as director and teacher

    1. Individualized lessons suited to each person's needs

    2. Dealing with the past, present and future

C. Jesus, the Master Rebuilder, at work

    1. Using various tools and circumstances for refinement

    2. Appointing tests and trials to be overcome

    3. The transformation into a vessel of honor, prepared for good works

V. The Divine Process: Producing Overcomers

A. The practical application of overcoming principles in daily life

    1. Dealing with character variations and weaknesses

    2. The cross as the heart of God's method

B. Two planes in which the redeemed may live

    1. The carnal, flesh realm vs. the heavenly, Spirit realm

    2. The need for transformation through crucifixion

C. Entering the school of the Holy Spirit

    1. Thorough self-examination under the light of the Spirit

    2. The Lord's methods: refiner's fire, fuller's soap, chastening

    3. Applying the cross deeper and deeper

D. The result of perseverance

    1. Transformation into the attitudes of Jesus Christ

    2. Unbounded liberty and attainment in the Spirit realm

A. Conclusion: The testimony of being crucified with Christ, yet living by faith in Him.

Here are 30 thought-provoking questions for small groups or private study

1. What distinguishes the "high calling" in Christ Jesus from the common salvation?

2. How does one properly respond to God's invitation to take part in His kingdom administration?

3. What qualities must an individual possess to be chosen for a role in Christ's Millennial Reign?

4. In what ways will the Millennial Kingdom differ from the current world system?

5. How can we cultivate a deeper fellowship and experience with God, similar to that of Enoch, Noah, Abraham, and Job?

6. What is the significance of developing a prophetic capacity in our lives?

7. How does true prophecy differ from enticing words of human wisdom?

8. In what ways did Jesus experience the sufferings and temptations of mankind, and how does this relate to His role as our High Priest?

9. How does the Word proceed from the Father, through the Son, and onward through believers?

10. What does it mean to be "perfect" or spiritually mature, and how does this relate to God's requirements in each dispensation?

11. In what ways are the privileges and experiences of believers increasing with each passing dispensation?

12. Why is it considered a great condescension for Christ to take a Bride from among men?

13. What is the significance of the Bride making herself ready through righteous acts?

14. How can we discover and enter God's School of Preparation for our lives?

15. What role does the Holy Spirit play as our director and teacher in this process?

16. How does Jesus, as the Master Rebuilder, work in our lives to refine and prepare us?

17. What is the purpose of the tests and trials appointed by God in our lives?

18. How can we practically apply the principles of overcoming in our daily lives?

19. What is the significance of the cross in God's method of producing overcomers?

20. What are the characteristics of living in the carnal, flesh realm versus the heavenly, Spirit realm?

21. Why is transformation through crucifixion necessary for believers?

22. How can we enter the school of the Holy Spirit and submit to His refining process?

23. What methods does the Lord use to refine and purify His people, and what is the purpose of each?

24. How can we apply the cross deeper and deeper in our lives, and what are the challenges we may face in doing so?

25. What are the benefits of persevering through the refining process and allowing God to transform our character?

26. How does transformation into the attitudes of Jesus Christ impact our lives and relationships?

27. What does it mean to experience unbounded liberty and attainment in the Spirit realm?

28. How can we live out the testimony of being crucified with Christ, yet alive in Him?

29. What steps can we take to awaken from spiritual slumber and heed Christ's call to maturity?

30. In what ways can we cooperate with the divine process of becoming overcomers and preparing to be part of Christ's Bride?

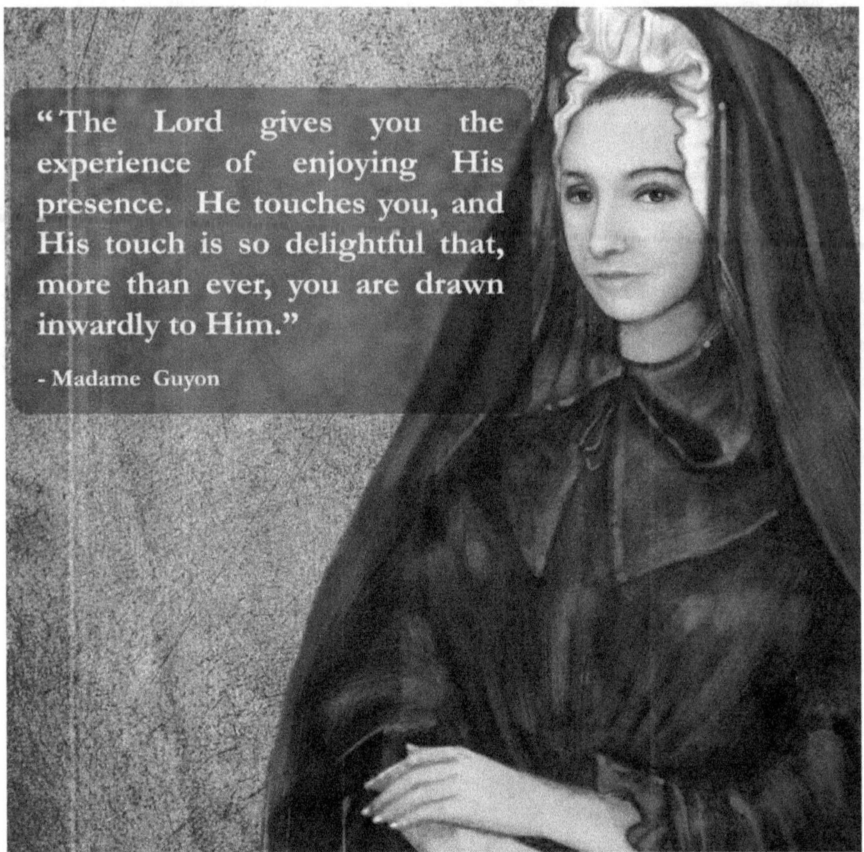

Madame Jeanne Guyon (1648-1717) was a French mystic and influential spiritual writer. She was raised in aristocratic society but felt drawn to an exclusive devotion to God from a young age. She married at 16 and was widowed with three small children by age 28.

Guyon devoted the rest of her 40-year life to evangelism, writing, and philanthropy. She founded hospitals and traveled around France and Switzerland teaching people how to pray and lead holy lives, meeting mainly in private to avoid overt preaching. She sought complete union with God, feeling that He spoke and acted through her a vessel.

This brought her into conflict with the Catholic Church, which opposed her Quietist teachings and belief that anyone, including women, could attain intimacy with God through contemplative prayer. After years of intimidation, she was imprisoned for seven years, the last two in solitary confinement.

Even in prison Guyon continued writing spiritual commentaries and letters. Her most famous work is a 20-volume commentary on the Bible. She also wrote an autobiography and shorter works on prayer and drawing close to God.

After her release Guyon continued her ministry for 15 more years, patiently enduring illnesses while writing and praising God. She shared a decades long spiritual friendship and correspondence with Archbishop François Fénelon before graduating to heaven at age 69.

Guyon attained an exceptionally deep intimacy and oneness with God through prayer. Despite intense persecution, she tirelessly shared her experience of Christ's presence.   Many of the teachers within this book frequently reference her writings. She still has her share of enemies though who misunderstand her message. However, her writings remain influential for those seeking deeper union with God.

CHAPTER 6

JOURNEY TO THE HEART:
AN INVITATION TO SIMPLE PRAYER

By Madame Guyon

(1648 – 1717)

Edited for Today's Generation 2024 by Steve Porter

This text was translated into English and originally published in the 1853 book "Spiritual Progress, or Instructions in the Divine Life of the Soul from the French of Fenelon and Madame Guyon." Steve Porter excerpted a small portion of the book, gave it a new title, a fresh edit for the modern reader, and republished it as a new work.

The Author's Preface.

———

This short treatise was originally written simply for a few individuals who wanted to wholeheartedly love God. Many others wanted copies because of the benefit they got from reading the manuscript, so it was therefore published.

It retains its original simplicity while being edited to enhance understanding for today's reader. This guide does not judge how others worship the Lord but provides an easy roadmap to intimacy with Christ.

The entire goal is to encourage the body of Christ into an easy and comfortable way of loving and serving God effectively. This path is designed for beginners, not requiring extensive study, but sincerely desiring true devotion with the Lord.

Any unbiased reader will find a hidden spiritual blessing that will motivate them to seek the happiness we should all long for. In saying perfection is easily attained, "easily" refers to how readily God is discovered within. Some may quote "You will seek me and not find me," but God also promises "Seek and you will find." Of course, clinging to sin blocks God's presence, but sincerely forsaking sin and searching internally brings Him near.

Many see spiritual life as unrealistic and devout prayer impossible to attain. But envisioning a goal as easily achieved fuels bold and vigorous pursuit, while viewing it as difficult breeds despair and reluctance. This writing aims to depict the goodness, desirability, and accessibility of a deeper walk with God.

If we grasped God's eagerness to connect with us, we wouldn't envision false obstacles. Since He "did not spare his own Son" for us, how will

He not also give us all things? This requires only small courage and perseverance, which we already exert for temporal things, if not the "one thing needed."

Let no one dismiss this way without personally testing it through lived experience. Pursue this guide sincerely, gently, and ready to learn, not with a haughty know it all critique. It was written so you might fully devote yourself to God; receive it with an open heart. It has no intention but to invite the humble and childlike into the confidence of the Father's love, grieved by their distrust. With yearning for your salvation, seek only God's love here, and you will surely obtain it.

Without elevating our views higher than others, we simply declare the fruit of our experience and many others in following the Lord this way. Since this chapter focuses specifically on prayer, many matters are not addressed, though nothing herein should offend if read in the intended spirit. Experience of those who try this path in earnest will prove we have written the truth.

Holy Jesus, lover of simplicity and innocence, you take delight in dwelling with childlike hearts willing to become "little children." You alone can empower this work, imprinting it on hearts and leading readers to find you within, where you wait in the manger to receive our love and testify of yours. We lose these blessings by our own hands. But you, Lord Almighty, uncreated Love, silent and all-containing Word, can make yourself loved, known and enjoyed. I know you will do so through this little work belonging entirely, proceeding wholly, and tending solely to you!

1.

The Prayer Of The Heart

Everyone can pray. It's tragic that most people think they lack a calling to prayer. All are called to prayer, just as all are called to salvation.

Prayer is simply applying your heart to God and exercising internal love. Saint Paul urged praying constantly (1 Thessalonians 5:17). Jesus said to keep watch and pray always (Mark 13:33, 37). Thus all can and should practice prayer. Intimate prayer may be harder to attain, but what I recommend is not complex and difficult.

Let all pray. You should live by prayer like you live by love. "I counsel you to buy from me gold refined by fire so you may be rich" (Revelation 3:18). This gold is easily obtained, much easier than you think possible.

Come all you thirsty to the living waters, and don't waste time trying to satisfy yourself with things that can't quench you (John 7:37; Jeremiah 2:13). Come you starving souls that can't find nourishment and be filled! Come, worn down under burdens, and be uplifted! Come sick to the Great Physician, and don't hesitate because of the extent of disease - bring all infirmities to be healed!

Children, approach your Father who will embrace you with love. Lost sheep, return to your Shepherd. Sinners, come to your Savior. Even you uneducated ones who feel incompetent for intimate prayer are specially called and fit for it. Jesus calls everyone without exception.

But those without a heart cannot come, for love requires a heart. Do you lack a tender, receptive heart? Surrender yours to God now and begin a deeper walk with Him. What a precious gift that is.

All desiring intimate prayer can easily pray through the Holy Spirit's grace given freely to everyone. Prayer is the key to maturity, the sovereign good, delivering from sin and attaining Christlikeness. Walking constantly in God's presence is the singular means of becoming spiritually mature. "Walk before me and be thou perfect" (mature)

(Genesis 17:1). Only intimate prayer sustains unbroken divine presence with Him.

This is the prayer of the heart, surpassing routines and rituals. Unlike the intellect's narrow focus, heart-prayer remains freely open past all reasoning, interrupted only by distracting passions. Once tasting divine sweetness, no lesser pleasure intrudes.

Nothing proves simpler than to savor God's actual presence! He resides closer than we are to ourselves, more eager to give than we are to receive. This simple way follows effortlessly as breathing. However far or numb you may feel, in prayer you can move through life immersed in the Divine. What tragic neglect then, to leave such bounty unopened! I trust that with this simple yet powerful method, you will not.

2.

THE FIRST DEGREE OF PRAYER: Reflection.

(Praying the holy scriptures)

There are two key ways to introduce prayer. One is reflection: selecting inspirational passages, reading slowly to fully digest small sections, extracting key ideas before continuing. This deeply engages the mind and encourages a transformation from the carnal and earthly to a renewed, spiritual mind rooted in Christ.

Another way is to read and think about what you're reading. Pause often to really understand the ideas and think about how you can use them in your life. This helps you think more deeply about spiritual wisdom. Doing this regularly can help you develop a prayerful mindset.

Taking time to quietly pray and think about God is very powerful. When you sit quietly and feel God's presence around you, it helps your mind and heart grow. Then, think deeply about scripture, not by trying to break it down, but by letting the Holy Spirit give you understanding.

Imagine Jesus right in front of you and feel Him deep inside your heart. This helps you ignore the distractions around you and focus on the holy place inside you where He lives. By focusing yourself this way, you can get closer to the Lord. **St. Augustine said that we waste a lot of time by not seeking God first in prayer.**

Once you focus inward and pull your thoughts away from distractions, everything becomes simpler. You can feel God's sweet presence and understand His truths, not by analyzing them, but by letting them fill your heart and strengthen your faith.

When you feel a strong passion for truth, revelation, and love, take a moment to rest and let those feelings grow inside you. Just like your body needs to digest food properly, your soul needs time to absorb spiritual nourishment. This slow and steady approach helps you grow spiritually more effectively than rushing through it.

149

As you continue to pray and focus inward, gently bring any wandering thoughts back to stillness. Trying to force distractions away can be hard, but by focusing on your faith, you can naturally let go of diversions. Stay aware that you are connecting with God's truth.

This first step of focusing inward and simplifying can be hard, especially if your mind is used to being busy all the time. But if you are willing to take a break from these old habits, you will soon find the inward path becoming smoother, with God's grace helping you on your journey into deeper intimacy.

3.

The Method of Prayer for Those Who Cannot Read

Those who cannot read books are not excluded from prayer simply because of that. The Holy Word which teaches all things, written all over within and without, is Jesus Christ Himself.

The method they should practice is this:

First, we should learn an important truth: "the kingdom of God is within you" (Luke 17:21). This means you should look for the Lord inside your heart. Just like teachers help you learn about God, teachers and pastors should teach people how to pray, not just about the reasons God created them. It's important to know why God made us, but it's just as important to know how to get closer to Him.

They should learn to start by sensing a deep awe and sweet surrender before God. Close your physical eyes and try to open the eyes and ears of your heart that the Lord may speak to you in His still small voice. Focus solely on Jesus Christ and let your love go before Him. Then, gather your thoughts and, with strong faith that Christ is within you, focus on His divine presence. Try to keep your senses and thoughts under control and not let them wander.

2. They should then recite the Lord's Prayer in their native language, reflecting a little on the meaning of the words and the infinite willingness of the God who dwells in them to truly become "their father." In this state let them lay out their needs before Him; and when they have said the word "father," remain a few moments in respectful silence, waiting to discern His voice.

Again, the Christian, seeing himself as a feeble child, defiled and badly wounded from repeated falls, lacking strength to stand or power to clean himself, should reveal his pitiable state plainly to his Father, occasionally mixing in a word or two of love and grief for ones sins and habits that have hurt the Lord's heart repeatedly and then sinking into quietness before Him. Then, continuing the Lord's Prayer, let him plead for this King of

151

Glory to reign in him, humbly repenting and surrendering himself so God may do so, while acknowledging God's right to rule over him.

If they feel drawn to peace and silence, they should not keep repeating the words of the prayer for as long as this sensation continues. When it passes, they may go on with the second petition, "Thy will be done on earth as it is in heaven!", whereupon these humble petitioners should beseech God to accomplish all His will in them and through them, and they should hand over their hearts and freedom into His hands, to dispose of as He pleases. When they feel the desire to love, they should ask for God's love. This should be done gently and calmly.

They don't need to worry about repeating set prayers too often. Even saying the Lord's Prayer once, in the way I described, can be very powerful and fruitful.

3. At other times, they may place themselves as sheep before their Shepherd, looking up to Him for their true nourishment: "O Divine Shepherd, You feed Your flock with Your very Self, and are indeed our daily bread." They can also lay before Him the needs of their families. But let all be done from this main and overarching viewpoint of faith, that God is inside them.

All our reflections about the Lord are not enough; a strong faith in His divine presence is what really matters. We shouldn't try to picture God, but it's okay to imagine Jesus Christ, such as during His birth or crucifixion. Always remember to seek Him in the center of your own soul. He resides within you in the great cathedral of your heart.

At other times, we can think of Jesus as a healer and give Him all our troubles for His loving, healing touch. But do this calmly, taking pauses now and then so that the quiet moments can last longer. This way, our effort becomes less, and by continually letting God work within us, He eventually takes full control, which will be explained later.

When we feel God's presence and start to enjoy the silence and stillness, this brings our soul into the second level of prayer. By following the steps

I've described, anyone can reach this level, whether they are educated or not. Some fortunate people even experience it right from the beginning.

4.

The Prayer of Simplicity

I want to write about "Stillness," or "The Prayer of Simplicity." I'll use "The Prayer of Simplicity" as it best describes the state we are discussing, which is not an advanced one.

After practicing the previous method for some time, the soul gradually finds it easier to approach God. It becomes less difficult to focus, making prayer easy, sweet, and delightful. The soul recognizes this as the true path to finding God and feels "his name is as ointment poured forth" (Song of Songs 1:3). The method must now change to the following, which must be pursued with courage and commitment, despite any difficulties encountered.

1. As soon as the soul, through faith, places itself in God's presence and becomes focused before Him, it should remain in respectful silence for a while. If, at the start, while making the act of faith, it feels a slight and pleasing sense of His presence, stay there without seeking any other focus and go no further, carefully cherishing this sensation as long as it lasts. When it fades, gently rouse the will with some tender affection. If this brings back a sweet peace, stay in that state. The fire of God's presence must be gently stoked, but once it is lit, stop all efforts lest activity extinguish it.

2. I strongly advise never finishing prayer without remaining afterward for some time in respectful silence.

3. It is also extremely important to come to prayer with courage and a pure, selfless love that seeks nothing from God but to please Him and do His will. A servant who works only for the hope of reward deserves none. Come to prayer not seeking spiritual delights, but only desiring to please God. This mindset will keep your spirit calm in both dry and joyful times, and will help you not be surprised by God's apparent absence.

5.

Afterword

In conclusion, Madame Guyon's treatise, "Journey to the Heart: An Invitation to Simple Prayer," serves as a powerful reminder that the path to a deep, intimate relationship with God is accessible to all. Regardless of one's level of education or spiritual experience, the door to prayer and divine communion remains open, beckoning us to enter.

Through her gentle guidance, Madame Guyon encourages us to embrace the simplicity and comfort of a life centered on loving and serving God. She dispels the misconception that prayer is a complex or burdensome task, reserved only for the most spiritually advanced. Instead, she presents it as a natural, effortless act of turning our hearts toward the One who longs to embrace us with His love.

Whether through the practice of being still in His presence, praying the Holy Scriptures, or the Prayer of Simplicity, Madame Guyon emphasizes the importance of sincerity, devotion, and a willingness to surrender our hearts to God's transformative presence. By offering practical methods and heartfelt encouragement, she invites us to embark on a journey of spiritual discovery, assured that God Himself will guide and empower us along the way.

As we internalize the truths presented in this chapter, we come to understand that the Kingdom of God lies within us, waiting to be discovered and cultivated through the simple act of intimate prayer. By stilling ourselves in His presence, relinquishing our attachments to worldly distractions, and allowing the fire of divine love to consume us, we open ourselves to the profound joy and peace that can only be found in communion with our Father.

Madame Guyon's words serve as a timeless reminder that the spiritual life is not a distant, unattainable goal, but a present reality, available to all who seek it with a sincere and devoted heart. Through her own experience and the testimonies of countless others who have walked this path, she assures us that the fruits of a life steeped in intimate prayer are truly transformative, leading us into an ever-deepening relationship with the Lord Jesus Christ.

As we conclude this chapter, let us take to heart the invitation extended by Madame Guyon to embark on a journey of simple, heartfelt prayer. May we approach this path with courage, commitment, and a childlike trust in the Father who longs to reveal Himself to us in the depths of our being. And may we, like countless saints and seekers before us, discover the untold riches and transformative power that await those who surrender themselves wholly to the love and guidance of our wonderful Lord!

Outline of Madame Guyon's "Journey to the Heart: An Invitation to Simple Prayer"

1. The Prayer of the Heart

- Universal Call to Prayer

  - Everyone can pray; it is a common misconception that prayer requires a special calling.

  - All are called to prayer just as all are called to salvation.

  - Prayer is simply applying your heart to God and exercising internal love.

- Scriptural Basis for Constant Prayer

  - Saint Paul urges praying constantly (1 Thessalonians 5:17).

  - Jesus commands to keep watch and pray always (Mark 13:33, 37).

- Prayer as Essential as Love

  - Prayer should be as integral to life as love.

  - **"I counsel you to buy from me gold refined by fire so you may be rich"** (Revelation 3:18) – this gold is easily obtained.

- Invitation to All

  - Come to the living waters and be filled.

  - Seek spiritual nourishment and healing.

  - Approach God as children to a loving Father.

  - Everyone is called, including those who feel unworthy or uneducated.

- Heart Requirement for Prayer

  - Love requires a tender, receptive heart.

  - Surrender your heart to God for a deeper walk with Him.

- Prayer through the Holy Spirit

- Intimate prayer is accessible to all through the Holy Spirit's grace.

  - Prayer is the key to maturity and Christlikeness.

  - Constant prayer sustains divine presence.

- The Simplicity of Heart-Prayer

  - Surpasses routines and rituals.

  - Freely open to divine sweetness, not hindered by intellectual analysis.

  - God's presence is closer than we are to ourselves.

2. The First Degree of Prayer: Reflection

- Introduction to Prayer

  - Two key ways: reflection and reading with integrated reflection.

- Reflective Reading

  - Select inspirational passages and read slowly to digest and extract key ideas.

  - Encourages transformation to a renewed, spiritual mind.

- Integrated Reflection

  - Pause to understand and apply ideas in life.

  - Develops a prayerful mindset.

- Quiet Prayer Time

  - Feel God's presence and think deeply about scripture.

  - Imagine Jesus before you to focus inward and ignore distractions.

- Focusing Inward

  - Simplifies thoughts and strengthens faith.

  - Digest spiritual nourishment slowly for effective growth.

- Handling Distractions

  - Gently bring thoughts back to stillness and focus on faith.

- God's grace smooths the inward path over time.

3. The Method of Prayer for Those Who Cannot Read

- Universal Access to Prayer

  - Inability to read does not exclude one from prayer.

  - Jesus Christ is the great book teaching all things.

- Teaching Method

  - **"The kingdom of God is within you"** (Luke 17:21) – seek God inside your heart.

  - Teachers and pastors should guide in prayer, not just catechism.

- Sensing God's Presence

  - Start with deep awe and surrender before God.

  - Close physical eyes and open the heart's eyes and ears.

  - Focus on Jesus Christ and gather thoughts in strong faith.

- The Lord's Prayer

  - Recite and reflect on its meaning.

  - Lay out needs before God and wait in respectful silence.

  - Recognize oneself as a child before a loving Father.

- Further Reflection and Prayer

  - Seek God's will and surrender to Him.

  - Ask for God's love gently and calmly.

- Other Forms of Prayer

  - Think of Jesus as a healer and present troubles for His healing.

  - Embrace silence and stillness to deepen prayer.

- Faith and God's Presence

  - Strong faith in God's presence matters more than visualizing Him.

- Imagine Jesus in various states to feel connected.

- Seek God in the soul's center.

4. The Prayer of Simplicity

- Introduction to Stillness

  - "The Prayer of Simplicity" best describes this state.

- Gradual Ease in Approaching God

  - Over time, prayer becomes easier and more delightful.

  - Recognize this as the true path to finding God.

- Method of Simplicity

  - Place yourself in God's presence and remain in respectful silence.

  - Cherish the sense of His presence without seeking other focuses.

  - Rouse the will with tender affection if the sensation fades.

- Post-Prayer Silence

  - Always remain in respectful silence after prayer.

- Courage and Selfless Love

  - Approach prayer with courage and pure, selfless love.

  - Seek to please God without desiring rewards.

  - This mindset keeps the spirit calm in both dry and joyful times.

5. Afterword

- Madame Guyon's Invitation to Simple Prayer

  - Path to deep, intimate relationship with God is accessible to all.

  - Prayer is not complex or burdensome.

- Embracing Simplicity and Comfort

- Encourages loving and serving God with sincerity.

- Methods of Prayer

- Being still in His presence, praying the Holy Scriptures, and the Prayer of Simplicity.

- Key Takeaways

- The Kingdom of God lies within us, discoverable through intimate prayer.

- Spiritual life is a present reality for those who seek it sincerely.

- Encouragement to Embark on Prayer Journey

- Approach with courage, commitment, and childlike trust.

- Discover the riches and transformative power of surrendering to God's love and guidance.

Here are 30 thought-provoking questions for small groups or private

1. How might viewing spiritual growth as easily attainable change one's approach to faith?

2. What obstacles do people commonly perceive in developing a deeper prayer life?

3. How does the author's description of prayer as "applying your heart to God" differ from traditional notions of prayer?

4. In what ways can the practice of constant prayer transform daily life?

5. How might focusing on God's eagerness to connect with us change our perspective on spiritual disciplines?

6. What role does humility play in developing a meaningful prayer life?

7. How can one balance the intellectual aspects of faith with the heart-centered approach described in the chapter?

8. What are the potential benefits and challenges of practicing "the prayer of the heart"?

9. How might the concept of God residing closer to us than we are to ourselves impact our understanding of spirituality?

10. In what ways can reading scripture reflectively enhance one's prayer life?

11. How does the author's approach to scripture reading differ from academic study?

12. What are the potential benefits of imagining Jesus present during prayer?

13. How might the practice of inward focus and simplicity in prayer affect other areas of life?

14. What role does patience play in developing a deeper prayer life?

15. How can those who cannot read engage in meaningful prayer according to the author?

16. What is the significance of understanding "the kingdom of God is within you" in the context of prayer?

17. How might reciting the Lord's Prayer in the manner described by the author change one's experience of it?

18. What is the importance of silence and pauses in prayer according to the chapter?

19. How does the author's description of faith differ from intellectual belief?

20. What are the potential benefits and challenges of seeking God in "the center of your own soul"?

21. How might the concept of God taking "full control" in prayer challenge or comfort different individuals?

22. What is the significance of approaching prayer with "courage and a pure, selfless love"?

23. How might the idea of not seeking spiritual delights in prayer change one's approach to spiritual disciplines?

24. What role does persistence play in developing the prayer of simplicity?

25. How might the practice of remaining in "respectful silence" after prayer impact one's spiritual life?

26. What are the potential benefits and challenges of viewing prayer as a "natural, effortless act"?

27. How does the author's approach to prayer challenge traditional religious practices?

28. What role does surrender play in the prayer methods described in the chapter?

29. How might the concept of the "Prayer of Simplicity" be applied in a busy, modern lifestyle?

30. In what ways does the author's approach to prayer potentially democratize spiritual growth?

CHAPTER 7
"MINISTRY UNTO THE LORD"

By Steve Porter

165

THE STORY

Prepare for a powerful journey inspired by Gabe Hoffman's touching piece "The Door to God's Heart" as revealed to him through prayer. This adaptation by Steve Porter is brought to you with a fresh perspective, originally shared in a live session by him and later polished for written publication.

Heavenly Father, I pray that You would bless these words and reveal Your presence and truth through them. Guide those reading to understand Your call on their lives. For those unsure of their path, make Your will clear so they can walk in the destiny You have for them. Transform hearts and minds to follow You. I thank You for opening the eyes of so many to see the vast variety of new directions and purposes You have laid out for them as they read. May You be glorified. Amen.

Imagine the Lord summoning you before His throne. You stand in the manifest presence of the Father and He tells you it's time to choose your heavenly calling. Confused, you turn to Him and ask, "Father, what would you have for me? What good could I do You?"

To this, the Father responds, "It is your choice. As my son or daughter, I will bless whatever you choose. But remember to choose wisely. Many before you have made hasty, impulsive decisions, leading them to shipwreck their lives. Choose carefully."

"Father, I desire to please You," you reply. "I want my life to play out like a beautiful melody for You. Ignite my heart to passionately seek You with my whole being. Attune my spirit to You as a violin to the Master's bow. Draw forth my life as an instrument for Your glory. What would you have me do?" He beckons for you to follow Him. Hand in hand, you cross the throne room and enter a narrow door leading to a long hallway. Lanterns light the corridor on both sides as you walk.

Eventually, you reach a door next to a table bearing oils. Inscribed on the door is the word "Healing". The Lord says, "This is a healing ministry, and you may choose to enter. I will empower you to bring about significant healings among the flock, if you choose to do so. This ministry is special and brings me immense joy, especially when the gift of healing is properly stewarded."

Glancing at the door, you notice a worn path created by multitudes who chose this gift. Intrigued, you say, "Lord, I want to choose this one, but I'm curious to know if there's more."

Smiling, He replies, "Follow me."

You continue down the corridor and encounter another door. Next to this door is a table with Elijah's staff, and the door reads "Miracles". The Lord says, "If you choose this ministry, I will use you to perform powerful miracles. You'll raise the dead, cast out demons, and heal diseases such as cancer and leukemia. The blind will see and the deaf will hear. I take great delight when my sons and daughters choose this ministry, as long as they steward it well."

This intrigues you, and you think, *I would love to be used to perform miracles. This is a powerful ministry.* Again, you notice the multitude of footprints leading into this room. Many who came before you have walked through that door, proclaiming, Miracles, that's my ministry!

Continuing down the path, you feel a deepening sense within you, an inner calling that there's more, something profound and everlasting. This hunger within you grows as you approach a third door. Adjacent to this door is a table holding John the Baptist's sandals. The word "Prophecy" is etched into the door. The Lord tells you, "I need prophets, especially in these end times. I need Holy Ghost-filled prophets, a mouthpiece, someone who will speak for Me. This is a potent ministry. Through the office of a prophet, I can change the course of Church history. This is a wise choice."

Looking at the Lord, you respond, "Lord, I would love to be a prophet, to speak Your words, to relay what's on Your heart. Yet, I know there's something more still to come. I know I need to go deeper." The Lord smiles at your words and tells you to follow Him. You continue to tread down the path.

Next, you encounter a door with a table beside it and on that table is a trumpet. The word "Evangelism" is inscribed on the door. The Lord explains, "I need those who will gather souls. Evangelists who will seek and save the lost, those burdened for the perishing and the ones bound for hell. This is an influential ministry."

While you're ready to say, "Yes, this is it," a strong presence continues to pull you down the path. Curiosity sparks within you. Asking the Lord once again if there's more, He leads you further down the path.

Next, you come across another table bearing scrolls, and on the door is the word "Teaching". You think, *This is it! I've always wanted to be a teacher, to break down the Word of God, to feed people, to stir them, teach them elementary things and lead them into the deeper mysteries of God. This must be the one.*

But then drums begin beating in the distance, their rhythmic pounding stirring something deep within. *What could those drums portend?* you wonder as yearning for more swells up inside you. "There must be more than being an educator," you muse hopefully. Bolstered with newfound resolve, you call upon the Lord to guide your steps along this mystifying path, wherever it may lead. With anticipation rising in sync with the drums' cadence, you press onward, determined to uncover whatever greater purpose might await you.

As the Lord smiles at you, you both continue walking hand in hand down the narrowing path. The further you go the darker it becomes. You notice that very few people venture this far as the doors here are not as grand, not as easily recognized or celebrated as the others. This part of the path is less travelled; it seems obscure and insignificant compared to the other options.

Upon reaching another door, you see the word "Love" inscribed on it. The Lord tells you, "I'm searching for those who will love mankind, who will love their brothers and sisters unconditionally. I'm looking for lovers of My precious people, those who will lay down their lives for My sheep."

You consider this carefully, thinking how beautiful it would be; yet the distant sound of drums keeps calling you, bidding you to continue further down the path. You decide to keep walking.

You then approach another door, the word "Intercession" etched into it. This door is noticeably darker, symbolizing the trials and tribulations an intercessor often grapples with. An intercessor's time is not their own; the Lord may come at inconvenient times, calling you to pray and intercede. If you choose to be an intercessor, you may need to say goodbye to peaceful, uninterrupted nights. On a side note, you might wonder why the Lord frequently calls upon intercessors. It's because there are so few of them on Earth.

Standing at the threshold of the door, the Lord says, "I am in need of intercessors, those who will pray on behalf of others, those who will wrestle in prayer until they witness a breakthrough. This is a very special ministry. Would you choose it?"

"Lord," you answer, "I long to be an intercessor for You. Yet within me, a deeper hunger stirs—one calling me to journey further by Your side." You reach for His outstretched hand. Together, you approach the final threshold.

"Very few choose this door," says the Lord, "for it leads down a path hidden from sight—one of ministering to My heart alone. Those who walk this way serve, love, worship, sing, and adore, ever laying themselves at My feet. Often misunderstood by others, they are urged to take on busier roles. Yet these beloved ones are My cherished Bride, a special remnant called to minister to Me and Me alone."

You gaze into the Lord's eyes, blazing like a divine fire, and declare, **"This is the ministry for me. I want to minister unto You."**

Hearing your heartfelt words, the Lord begins to weep. Tears roll down His beautiful face, and instinctively you reach up to dry His tears. Apologizing for your quick action, you say, "Lord, I'm sorry—"

He gently interrupts you. "My son, my daughter, you will do that many times." Then, with a joyful look, He continues, "These are tears of joy, for you have chosen to minister unto Me."

With your declaration, you walk through the door. As you cross its threshold, you see David, Enoch, Abraham, John the Beloved, and other holy figures. They all rush toward you to welcome you, and you express surprise at their attendance. To this, they respond, "What do you think we've been doing through all the ages? We've been ministering unto the Lord!"

With tears still gleaming in His eyes, the Lord hands you a golden key. He tells you, "This key will open every other door. Because you have chosen to minister unto Me, I will now use you in every other way—miracles, prophecies, evangelism, teaching, love, intercession. But you will go forth in My power and in My love, for you have chosen the greatest path!"

All praise to Jesus, for all lesser ministries blossom within this greater calling. Hallelujah!

My Journey

The Lord has been gently guiding me for many years towards ministering unto Him. My heart sings with joy, for I believe this purpose is what Diane and I are called to fulfill—to directly serve the sweet Lord Himself. The allure of other flashy titles faded long ago as we walked with our Best Friend in the garden. This journey was never meant to be about acclaim or status in the eyes of man. Rather, the drums' rhythmic pulse in this story reflects the very heartbeat of the Father. As we attune ourselves to its heavenly sound through lingering in His presence, we learn to discern the tender whispers of His heart.

The call resounds. "Draw near, beloved ones. Listen and understand what the Spirit is saying. Serve Me out of the overflow of our sacred times together." Oh, to minister to the Lord Himself! This highest privilege leaves me undone. To gaze upon His beauty, to sit at His feet, to let my worship fill the air as I drench His feet with my tears—here is the place of deepest fulfillment. As He shares the secrets of His heart, mine overflows in adoring devotion. Out of this holy exchange, His purposes unfold. What wondrous intimacy! What glorious service! The drums beat on, stirring this Bride's affection for the Bridegroom.

Come then, precious friend. Let us meet with Him in the secret garden and tenderly minister to our Love. I am confident that not only am I called to minister unto the Lord but also that our gatherings and ministry are intended to nurture those with the same yearning––to serve Him alone. This purpose stirs my deepest passion, even moving me to many tears. I am profoundly touched envisioning a ministry wholly devoted to Christ Himself, raising up others who will likewise adore Him. The Lord surely blesses every form of service, yet what touches His heart most deeply is the choice to minister to Him personally. Of all pathways that move Him, the door into His intimate presence is the one He treasures beyond all else. Those who simply come to Him, to selflessly love and worship their Savior––those He can trust with more.

My dear friends, there are some who focus exclusively on healings and miracles. That's all they talk about, and while that's wonderful—and I myself have been lifted from my deathbed by the Lord many times, surviving fatal diseases and countless attempts by Satan to take my life—there is something more. Something deeper awaiting us. You can become enamored with the acts and hand of God and never truly connect with His heart.

That is why some will stand before Him in heaven and recite, "Did I not perform wonders? Did I not accomplish great feats in Your name?" Yet the Lord will mournfully reply, "I never sanctioned such deeds. **I did not know you at all**" (Matthew 7:22–23).

We may be utilized in miracles, anointed despite our frailty. But if we remain strangers to the Savior, it proves insufficient. More vital than signs and wonders, more meaningful than prolific ministry, is our ability to develop a closeness where we hear His very heartbeat. Beyond imparting truth, beyond proclaiming salvation, beyond proclaiming prophetic insight, it's vital **to know and love Christ**. Our works are worthless when devoid of love for the Lord Himself.

When we minister unto the Lord, dwelling in His presence, attuned to His heartbeat, it naturally follows that we are empowered from on high for every other noble work He may call us to. As we walk with our Best Friend, gazing into His eyes of fire, His glory rubs off on us. Out of the overflow of our extravagant worship and devotion to the Bridegroom, His power flows through us to minister to others. The anointing effortlessly falls upon us as we fall on our faces before Him. Yet the critical difference emerges here: **our gaze remains fixed on Christ alone**. As the author and perfecter of faith, He merits our focus. No longer distracted by the adversary, or only by miracles or manifestations, our sights stay rooted on Jesus. From this post, with our eyes lifted heavenward, we become conduits of His life flowing through us. As we abide in intimacy with Him, listening to His gentle whisper, we can readily shout His mighty deeds from the rooftops. Yet we continually return to that inner chamber––to once again minister to our Lord.

In recent days, a sacred invitation to a "Ministry unto the Lord" has profoundly stirred my spirit. My heart sings with this realization for I believe it captures the very purpose of Christ's Bride––to adore and serve her Groom with abandon. The lure of notoriety faded for His Bride long ago. This journey is not about spectacle or performance but about tender union with the Divine Creator. Our extravagant God seeks not only displays of power but also quiet wells of living water offered in love. The One through who all was spoken into being now bids His beloved, "Speak to Me." And in that whisper, we discover our true calling. A high calling with no guile.

The pulsing drums in our story are the very heartbeat of the Father reverberating through our hearts––guiding us to our one true calling. Though only perceived by some, these heavenly rhythms echo all around us. As we gather to meet with Jesus in the quiet garden, we attune our hearts to the beautiful cadence of His. I firmly believe our calling as His cherished Bride is to model surrendered devotion at His feet until others echo the same wholehearted service of the King.

The pounding of the drums grows louder, awakening our spirits to the Bridegroom's passionate longing for us. **"Set me as a seal upon your heart,"** He cries. As we yield to the rhythm of His fiery love and goodness, this sacred stamp marks us as His very own. Then, filled with the same holy fire, we blaze through the darkness beckoning, "Come! Let your heartbeat synchronize with His. Taste and see His extravagant affection!"

This purpose ignites our passion, even moving many to tears. Envisioning a community devoted to Christ Himself, inspiring others to similar devotion, resonates with our deepest longing. Myriad pathways stretched before us, yet the door that truly touched His heart, that mirrored His own tears, was the one leading to deeper intimacy with Him. To minister unto the Lord remains the choice that resonates most profoundly with His Spirit.

In learning to minister unto the Lord, I've grasped the necessity of divine timing. In my early days, impatience drove me to forge ahead in my own strength. I remember writing hundreds of letters, inviting myself to any pulpit that would have me. My zeal abounded, yet my approach lacked wisdom; this is often seen today as many self-promote themselves on social media all day long without a true love and relationship with God. With me, out of all those appeals, only one opened its door––without lasting fruit.

But when the Lord sends out His faithful ones, the story unfolds differently. First, He bids, "Come deeper in. Know My heart." As we meet Him there in the secret place, He then says, "Now go forth where I send you." Founded not on programs but His presence, such gatherings soon blossom into communities, diverse yet united in adoration. They stream in from all directions, ignited by His Spirit to minister love to His Son. What begins as two or three is multiplied into a tapestry of ongoing worship. For it is always by His power, moving as He wills, that the Lord's house expands. Through yielded vessels the Master crafts His dwelling place.

We face a choice to walk in our own wisdom or His way. Do we want His path––to minister unto Him alone? This calls to mind the maiden of the vineyards from Song of Solomon's opening pages. (See Song of Solomon 1) Having labored long under the relentless sun to serve all but herself, fatigue overtook her form. Through this prophetic allegory, we glimpse one who poured out in charity until none remained for her own soul's care. Provoking the indignation of family who watched her stumble past the bounds of balance, still this noble young woman persevered.

Yet even the most righteous works, when unrestrained by wisdom, ultimately sap vitality reserved for our Beloved. Though well-intentioned, busyness that steals our gaze from our Lover's face inevitably wilts the garden enclosed for Him. There comes an hour when sweat-drenched brows signal a shift in season, uprooting misplaced vines to make room for deeper roots.

This parable beckons us––like the Shulamite––to nurture the soil of intimacy with Christ above all else. From that abiding place flows ministry unto Him and, in turn, unto others. How often we mirror her journey, immersed in worthy work yet famished in spirit! Busyness shrouds our eyes even amidst progress, blind to the creeping cracks beneath our feet. Yet the Lord in His mercy reveals this folly, calling His beloved ones back to the garden sealed for Him alone. There, in the quiet hush of His Presence, we discover serving springs sweetest when it overflows not from duty but adoration. As we steep ourselves in worship, the True Vine engrafts our hearts. Then, nourished by Source, we may pour out again to those in need.

To put it plainly, preoccupation with **doing** can eclipse our highest calling—ministering unto the Lord Himself. A vessel poured out too long soon runs dry. Without regularly retreating into His presence for rest, silent wonder, and listening at His feet, the wells of divine communion within us fade. In overextending through even virtuous service, we court spiritual famine. Like a garden denied rainfall while busily pulling weeds, our best efforts grow brittle and brown. Unchecked, this imbalance fans frustration's flames––often scorching our nearest loved ones, most of all family.

The Shulamite's cry, which pleads, **"My mother's children were angry with me; they made me the keeper of the vineyards, but my own vineyard have I not kept," (V.6)** echoes through the ages, strikingly familiar still. When spiritual nourishment fades, so too does the fruit of the Spirit within. Operating from duty and might rather than His depths of power, we court collision. Preoccupation with deeds, however well meant, cannot compensate for pantries left bare. Here the initial slip into seemingly harmless busyness takes its toll. Bit by bit, flames of affection cool without the oil of intimacy. What began as a choice rooted in serving man slowly shifts. Imperceptibly, vine by vine, it changes course until ministering unto God alone stands as a relic of another season.

A critical distinction exists between good endeavors and God-breathed ones. Not every worthy effort aligns with His tailored design for our lives. Wisdom urges caution; busyness has a tempting allure, promising purpose yet often pulling us from sacred shores. Before launching ships rendered for great voyages, we must first prepare the vessels. Our highest service comes not through filling calendars or marking off our to-do lists but from filling up on His divine presence––ministering unto the Lord who then sends out the twelve. From this flowing stream branches life's most fruitful deeds. That which is built when the Builder first dwells within holds up against crushing waves. Work woven through wordless worship bears eternal weight. The houses framed when abiding in the Cornerstone stand firm forever.

We are called to live led by the Spirit, reflecting His fruits through us. We are invited to abide in the Vine, bearing **much fruit** that will last the journey (John 15).

Today, a choice confronts us––what manner of ministry shall we embrace? I urge you toward the path less traveled, the road less publicly applauded, to minister unto Christ our Lord. For though subtle and unseen by men's admiring eyes, the Bridegroom Himself marks the depth of our devotion. From this sacred chamber, His secrets and strategies pour forth, fueling words that transform. As the faithful ones tend to His wounds of longing, healing liquid love, He––in this intimacy––makes our faces to shine like the dawn. Then, as Revelation's Bride adorned for her Husband, we emerge filled with His splendor.

They are the "Overcomers", Revelation's faithful band––devoted unto the Lord despite the age's raging storms. To safeguard this holy calling, wisdom urges caution in our scheduling. Without mindful rhythm, days become a dizzying merry-go-round––hence choices confront us by design, not default, and we must shape our hours. That which ultimately does not nourish our bond with the Bridegroom must give way for a season. I myself have stumbled there, dashing about while inwardly parched––ever moving externally yet internally malnourished. How I dislike the hollow hustle devoid of abiding grace! Instead, I yearn for courts of joy where souls are lovingly replenished.

Before tending another's vine, let me first nurture my orchard enclosed for the King. For only from fullness of spirit arrives ministry overflow––the secret unlocking everlasting fruit. Hallelujah! From the abundance dwelling inside, rivers now flow.

Song of Solomon 7:11–12 illuminates this truth. **"<u>Come, my beloved</u>, <u>let us go</u> forth into the field. Let us lodge in the villages. Let us get up early to the vineyards, let us see if the vine flourish, whether the tender grapes appear and the pomegranates bud forth. There will I give thee my love."** <u>Come</u>, my beloved, let us <u>go</u> to the vineyards and villages; see if blossoms grace the vine." A vital principle emerges in verse 11: **"<u>Come</u> before you <u>go</u>."**

First, we are beckoned deeper into intimacy, meeting with our Love in stillness. From this overflowing Oasis––saturated in His presence through lingering worship––proceeds all fruitful work. As we sing new songs over Him alone, drink deep from wells of living water, then and only then can we "go forth into the field" or "lodge in the villages."

Oh beloved, do you yearn in your innermost being to dwell where the Master desires? Does your heart ache to embark on holy quests, sent as His ambassador where no other dares to go? If so, pause first to heed the gentle call of the Spirit**: "Come away, My love."** Feel His soothing summons beckoning you into sacred depths—**"Come to Me, you weary one, and drink freely from rivers of rest."**

Envision now the courts of Heaven, resplendent in jasper and ruby, where we meet the Strength-Giver and Sweet Master. Here we lay down feeble human efforts, exchanging striving for currents of grace gushing from another realm. As we minister to Him in tender adoration, so too He ministers renewal into the depths of our being–– replenishing an empty soul with treasure troves from Heaven's storehouses. These polished jewels and shimmering gems, refined in worship's crucible, recast our common lives into carriers of God's glory! We are transformed not by human straining but by divine inflow. Thus prepared and equipped by surrender, we proceed strengthened for the mission. From the overflow of His unconditional extravagance wells up rivers of new wine, new oil, new life––washing the dust of the ages from a dry and thirsty land.

Can you hear it, beloved? Listen closely to the whisper of the Spirit—the Father's tender invitation extending to you even now: **"Come away, come away with Me...."** Like a Lover beckoning His Bride, He calls you by name, wooing your heart to draw near. **"Come, My beloved, come and lodge deep in fields of intimacy where I dwell."**

In this secret garden flows the oil of intimacy empowering all noble work. Here the distinctions between platform and prayer closet fade into oneness. For I tell you a mystery: the life flowing through the one ministering springs from the same Source, filling the silent adorer alone with her Lord.

Long ago, I asked the Master to birth equal joy within me for both public gatherings and my private chamber where none but Jesus hears the secrets and worship I pour at His feet. And He granted this request, nurturing a depth of satisfaction unlike any other as I retreat into love's sanctuary. After preaching stirs hungry souls, joy meets me in the holy chambers. Here in stillness with the Beloved my reserves are lovingly replenished.

Here I await the next holy assignment, embracing rest between adventures bathed in Presence. Hidden in His pavilion I prepare for commissioning, filled to overflow for the next assignment. Empowered anew through lingering in each other's gaze, soon we will sally forth again hand in hand. But for now, stillness and extravagant adoration reside in the haven of His heart.

Beloved, this sacred call into the depths of God's heart spans beyond preachers behind pulpits. It echoes and resounds within each longing spirit! Together we cross the threshold into love's inner chamber, to sit at His feet and await holy assignments perfectly crafted for our lives.

In these encounters, the Master personally hands us keys, granting access to the precise doors He has prepared. We proceed not by the strength of the flesh but through unlocking realms in the Spirit gifted by Him.

There may come appointed times when the Lord tenderly urges you to teach truth imparted through intimacy. Miracles will effortlessly confirm the message as hungry hearts receive the bread you faithfully deliver. On certain days, while walking familiar streets, the same Spirit may highlight strangers to bless––divine appointments to pray, seeing captives freed, bodies healed, destinies restored at His Word. You may suddenly prophesy treasures from a throne room encounter still echoing deep within.

Yet the difference emerges not from chosen paths but surrendered vessels through which rivers of life flow. First comes stillness before the King, gazing in wonder as we drink our fill of His presence. Here in chambers of rest, the Master renews feeble mortal strength with might and divine power. Only then, prepared and steadied, we march forth at His command.

"Let us get up early"—what does "early" mean? It indeed implies the beginning of the day, but it also means **"first."** In other words, I'm going to give You, Jesus, **the first priority**. I won't merely slot You into an empty space in my schedule; instead, I will make myself available to the Lord always.

How well I know those sudden moments when the Lord's consuming presence sweeps over me unexpectedly! During times when driving down familiar roads, the Spirit has overwhelmed me to the point of pulling aside––moved to intercede with tears for towns I passed through.

The Lover of my soul arrives unannounced, heeding neither clocks nor comfort. In the deep still of night, as weariness weighs heavily, the voice I know so well rouses me from dreams. Despite pleas for "five more minutes," love propels me from slumber into holy exchange once again.

I vow to make Him my sole priority, above all other earthly comforts and claims on my time. This means answering the Bridegroom's summons at inconvenient moments, interrupting well-laid plans ... because He is worth any sacrifice. As we persevere in answering the cry of "Come away!" slowly He entrusts us with more and more depth of intimate friendship. We join the ranks of history's "friends of God"—the Moseses and Enochs who walked in sweet intimacy of exchange well beyond the veil. All Heaven leaned in to eavesdrop as they conversed face-to-face with the Great I AM.

Like John the Beloved resting upon His chest, if we linger long enough in stillness, we too hear secrets from the Master's quarters. We become entrusted friends of the Most High, invited within the circle of God's personal confidence. But it starts by saying yes to the whisper. **"Come."**

I sense the Lord saying, "Arise, cleave to Me in the dawning, come away to green pastures still heavy with dew.... There in tenderness we will linger until daylight breaks fully within. Come see the vine flourishing under summer's warm kiss, the grapes grown plump, almost bursting with the new wine I pour out. Do you wish to drink freely from measures pressed and overflowing as you receive more of My extravagant Love?"

Oh beloved, is there anything more heavenly than meeting His "I love you" with our own heart's echo resounding, "I love You too, Lord!" To not simply say thanks but to stop and let thankfulness swell into equally lavish adoration until He sees the reflection of His own affection gazing back. After the Master speaks such tender words, let us risk being still longer instead of springing to the next thing. Let His declaration find a resting place to marinate until He finds your gaze again. Drink in the wine of His presence until the fullness of joy reveals that we are truly, fully, absolutely loved in a manner no mind conceived before this divine appointment.

Once in a dream, suddenly I found the Lord Himself sitting beside me within the close confines of my ordinary vehicle. His gaze burned with a fiery affection I had only glimpsed from afar before this unexpected encounter.

Drawing on courage, I turned fully toward Him. "I want to know You more." The words tumbled out unplanned.

Instantly He replied, "You can. For I am always right here with you, Steve."

In that moment, words faded into the background. I leaned upon His chest and felt a depth of love no language could approach. Wave after wave of Spirit communion washed between us as my entire soul cried out in a resounding chorus, "I love You, Jesus!" His reciprocal reply cascaded through every fiber of my being until human containers could scarcely hold such sacred exchange. I emerged forever changed in that life-defining moment.

Oh beloved, there remains no sweeter place than the depths of night, when the world's clamor dies down and we simply linger overwhelmed by His presence! What greater ministry than to pour out the oil of adoration upon His feet? When His manifest nearness arrives, no fear can stand. Suddenly He is so tangibly near, if we reach out our hands––like Thomas––and touch living flesh and pulsing heart. The vivid intensity surpasses words and invites inward prostration. He leans in close enough for us to feel the warmth of His breath, closer than any embrace, nearer than understanding. Our own breath catches in recognition. Here, beautifully manifest, is our very Father who longs for our company.

As we close our time together, a holy invitation beckons each hungry heart to cross a pivotal threshold. What I wouldn't give for you beloved ones to taste and see His goodness (Psalm 34:8), to enter His courts (Psalm 65:4) and behold firsthand the unparalleled glories of ministering unto the Lord alone! A choice now emerges: which door of service calls you by name? Of many worthwhile paths indeed, one leads where few ever venture, speaking mysteries of surrender and reward cascading down through the ages.

Those courageous and yearning few who choose to abandon themselves wholly to extravagant adoration find themselves flooded with a revelation of Jesus so profoundly deep it sets their souls forever ablaze. Further and further in He draws you until Earth's shadows fade completely within the brilliance now resonating through His Bride. Every encounter becomes inches from His face instead of moments in passing. This relinquishing invites lavish reward––as every tiny act of devoted affection elicits even more from the Groom's heart in return.

Suddenly from joy's lips pour rivers of living water Christ-followers long sought from vain dead cisterns (Jeremiah 2:13). These cherished ones carry the very heartbeat of God Himself now wherever feet may roam. People will be supernaturally drawn to you, seeking the illumination the Spirit exudes yet not realizing the Source is simply that hidden life of intimacy, which overflows from your intimate communion with the Lord.

A ministry unto Himself––the King's own sacred chamber where we may gaze upon and adore Him, letting everything else fade. This longing has resonated within me since first glimpsing His heart. Oh, the depths of satisfaction when at last your soul discovers its ultimate purpose for which it was crafted, simply to return unceasing, extravagant, all-out, never-ending AFFECTION back to its Maker! I tell you, all else pales in comparison to this profoundly fulfilling summons! Will you answer the sweet Master's invitation today?

Father, I lift up hands that hang helpless to orchestrate transformation of any eternal weight. Originator of life and breath, only You can touch each listening heart with a stunning invitation to the ultimate calling. Would Your Spirit cascade the depths of every soul under the sound of my voice or reading these engraved words? Compel a profound response within ... summon them to sacred chambers of encounter too few dare to enter! Make the choice clear, Beloved Lord. Send dreams and visions illuminating true desire. Unveil which paths lead to momentary rewards and which to crowns laid down at the Master's feet. I intercede for divine collision awakening passionate pursuit within each unique design and destiny unto intimate communion with Christ the Bridegroom.

Beloved Bride, the Lord bids you now to respond to His burning heart! Pause in a sacred space to engage this Suitor face-to-face. Within the joy-drenched mystery of the prayer closet, let Him hear the tender exchange of your own deepest devotion. Hold nothing back; conceal no secrets, tears or wrestling dreams from His gaze that locks unwaveringly upon you. There divulge your deepest longings and dwell within His all-consuming love.

O Ancient of Days, draw near Your children once more! Spark fiery desire and unsated hunger, compelling us hard upon the chase until we fling ourselves into Your tender embrace, love-sick forevermore! Expand these earthen vessels with capacity for more of Your vast abundance than mortal fabrics can contain! As Moses of old could not look upon the fullest revelation and live, shatter every limiting ceiling that we might risk equally perilous visions of Heaven's resplendence! Let not weariness diminish urgency until, as those who are fully known, we make the beloved Bridegroom our sole life's offering.

I charge you, my dear friend, to tenderly wipe His tears with worship as He pronounces, "It is enough."

The table is now prepared. Then He takes your hand in procession to the Marriage Feast, spilling forth lavish bounty, ringing with joyful laughter, flowing with new wine and mercy without measure.... Oneness consummated within the heart, His radiant Bride embraced forever in the sight of all.

The air is thick with anticipation as you walk hand in hand with the Beautiful One down the petal-strewn path to the banquet hall. The vines are heavy with ripe fruit; the roses fill the air with their perfume. Your Beloved turns to you, eyes dancing, and whispers, **"The wait is over, My love. Come, let us feast together."**

The Bridegroom has welcomed His Bride home. What glorious intimacy now, what a marvelous union! The drums keep pounding out: Yours is the Kingdom, the Power, and the Glory forever, O Ancient of Days!

On this holy day, we are overcome with joy that we have lived a life devoted to ministering unto our God alone. As we behold the smiling face of our beautiful Lord who first captivated our gaze, our hearts erupt in praise and grateful delight.

Joy unspeakable resounds as we realize the fulfillment of our highest calling—to love Him, to adore Him, to tend the garden with Him. "Worthy, worthy is the Lamb!" we cry. Worthy of our abandon, our extravagant affections, our wholehearted service and loyalty through all our days. He is worth it all! No words can capture the perfection of this moment. We have reached journey's end in the arms of the Lover of our souls. After all the seeking and longing, we are Home at last.

Outline of Steve Porter's "Ministry Unto the Lord"

Introduction

    A. Inspiration for Ministry Unto the Lord

    B. Prayer for God's blessing and revelation through the words

I. Empowerment to bring significant healings

    A. Standing before God's throne and being asked to choose a ministry

    B. The importance of choosing wisely

II. Many choosing this ministry

    A. The Door of Healing

        1. Empowerment to bring significant healings

        2. Many choosing this ministry

    B. The Door of Miracles

        1. Performing powerful miracles

        2. Raising the dead, casting out demons, and healing diseases

    C. The Door of Prophecy

        1. Being a mouthpiece for God, especially in the end times

        2. The potential to change the course of Church history

    D. The Door of Evangelism

        1. Gathering souls and seeking the lost

        2. An influential ministry

    E. The Door of Teaching

        1. Breaking down the Word of God and feeding people

        2. Leading others into the deeper mysteries of God

    F. The Door of Love

        1. Loving mankind and God's people unconditionally

  2. Laying down one's life for God's sheep

 G. The Door of Intercession

   1. Praying on behalf of others and wrestling in prayer

   2. A special ministry, but one with trials and tribulations

III. The Final Door: Ministering Unto the Lord

  A. A hidden path, chosen by few

  B. Serving, loving, worshiping, singing, and adoring God alone

  C. Often misunderstood by others

  D. God's cherished Bride and special remnant

IV. Choosing to Minister Unto the Lord

  A. The Lord's joyful response and tears

  B. Receiving a golden key that opens every other door

  C. Meeting other biblical figures who ministered unto the Lord

V. Steve Porter's Personal Journey

 A. The Lord's gentle guidance towards ministering unto Him

 B. The highest privilege and deepest fulfillment

 C. The importance of divine timing and God's sending

 D. The danger of self-promotion and busyness without true love for God

 E. The call to nurture intimacy with Christ above all else

 F. The distinction between good endeavors and God-breathed ones

VI. The Invitation to Minister Unto the Lord

 A. A choice between the path of acclaim and the path of devotion

 B. The call to meet with Jesus in the quiet garden

   C. The pounding drums as the Father's heartbeat, calling us to intimacy

   D. Becoming marked as God's own and blazing through darkness

   E. The importance of abiding in God's presence before going forth in ministry

   F. Becoming carriers of God's glory through worship and surrender

Conclusion

   A. The choice to answer the Bridegroom's summons at any moment

   B. Becoming entrusted friends of God through intimacy

   C. Experiencing the depths of God's love and presence

   D. A prayer for divine collision and awakening to passionate pursuit of Christ

   E. The call to make the Bridegroom our sole life's offering

   F. The anticipation of the Marriage Feast and the fulfillment of our highest calling

Here are 30 thought-provoking questions for small groups or private study

1. If you were standing before God's throne and asked to choose a heavenly calling, which ministry would you feel most drawn to, and why?

2. How can the importance of choosing wisely in ministry be applied to our daily decisions and priorities?

3. What are the potential dangers of pursuing a ministry solely based on its popularity or outward appearance of success?

4. How can we cultivate a heart that is more focused on ministering to God Himself, rather than seeking the approval or recognition of others?

5. In what ways can our own desires for significance or impact hinder us from fully embracing the call to minister unto the Lord?

6. How might our understanding of God's love and nature be transformed by spending more time in His presence, ministering to Him?

7. What are some practical ways we can integrate the practice of ministering unto the Lord into our daily lives and routines?

8. How can we discern the difference between God-breathed endeavors and good, but ultimately self-directed ones?

9. In what ways might our relationships and interactions with others change as we prioritize our relationship with God above all else?

10. How can we cultivate a deeper sensitivity to God's heartbeat and invitation to intimacy with Him?

11. What might it look like to be marked by God's presence and to blaze through darkness as a result of our devotion to Him?

12. How can we maintain a posture of abiding in God's presence, even in the midst of busy schedules and demands on our time and energy?

13. What are some of the challenges or obstacles that can hinder us from fully embracing the call to minister unto the Lord, and how can we overcome them?

14. How might our understanding of worship be expanded or deepened as we prioritize ministering to God above all else?

15. In what ways can our surrender to God and devotion to Him transform us into carriers of His glory and presence?

16. How can we cultivate a heart that is quick to respond to the Bridegroom's summons, even when it comes at inconvenient or unexpected times?

17. What might it look like to become entrusted friends of God through a life of intimacy and devotion to Him?

18. How can we create space in our lives for the kind of deep, transformative encounters with God's love and presence that Steve Porter describes?

19. In what ways might our lives and ministries be impacted by a genuine, passionate pursuit of Christ above all else?

20. How can we encourage and support one another in the journey of making the Bridegroom our sole life's offering?

21. What are some practical steps we can take to cultivate a lifestyle of ministering unto the Lord, both individually and in community with others?

22. How might our understanding of God's calling on our lives shift as we prioritize intimacy with Him above all else?

23. In what ways can we balance the call to minister unto the Lord with the responsibilities and demands of daily life and service to others?

24. How can we discern when God is calling us to step out in ministry to others, and when He is inviting us to focus primarily on ministering to Him?

25. What are some of the fruits or evidences of a life that is wholly devoted to ministering unto the Lord, and how might these be manifested in our own lives?

26. How can we cultivate a heart of extravagant love and devotion to God, even in the midst of a world that often prioritizes other things?

27. In what ways might our worship and adoration of God be transformed as we spend more time in His presence, ministering to Him?

28. How can we maintain a posture of humility and dependence on God, even as He entrusts us with greater measure of His presence and power?

29. What might it look like to live with a constant anticipation of the Marriage Feast and the ultimate fulfillment of our highest calling in Christ?

30. How can we encourage and inspire others to embrace the call to minister unto the Lord, and what impact might this have on the body of Christ as a whole?

CHAPTER 8
FINAL WORD

Dearly beloved friends, as we draw near to the close of this sacred journey, my heart overflows with gratitude for the privilege of walking alongside you through these pages. The lives and wisdom of the precious saints featured within---Wade Taylor, John Wright Follette, Hattie Hammond, Madame Guyon, Walter Beuttler, and Seeley Kinne---have left an indelible mark on my soul, igniting a deeper hunger for the Lord's presence and a resolute commitment to the higher calling of ministering unto Him alone.

Each author, in their unique way, has illuminated the path of abandoned devotion, inviting us to lay aside lesser pursuits and give ourselves wholly to the One who is worthy of our all. Their words, forged in the crucible of intimate communion with Christ, carry the weight of eternity---beckoning us to the secret place where the Beloved waits to ravish our hearts with His all-consuming love.

As I have pressed into their timeless insights, I have found my own spirit set ablaze with fresh passion for Jesus. The depths of Wade Taylor's revelatory teachings on the Bride's high calling, the poetic wisdom of John Wright Follette, the uncompromising conviction of Hattie Hammond, the gentle yet profound guidance of Madame Guyon, the infectious hunger for God's manifest presence embodied by Walter Beuttler, and the prophetic clarity of Seeley Kinne have woven together a tapestry of truth that has both captivated and transformed me.

Oh, how I long for you, dear reader, to be equally undone by the beauty of the Bridegroom as you tarry in His presence! May the Holy Spirit take these words and ignite them as living flames within your soul, compelling you to abandon yourself to the One who abandoned everything for us. Let us run together into the arms of our Beloved, allowing His fiery gaze to consume every lesser affection until only He remains.

In the end, may we be found as those who have chosen the better part---who have sat at the feet of Jesus, broken open the alabaster box of our lives, and poured out every ounce of our devotion as a fragrant offering before Him. May our lives become a blazing witness of the all-surpassing worth of knowing Christ Jesus our Lord, counting everything else as loss in comparison to the excellency of His knowledge.

Beloved, let us arise and shine, for our light has come! The glory of the Lord is rising upon us, and He is calling us to carry His presence to a world desperate for encounter. As we go forth from this place of consecration, may we do so as burning and shining lamps, reflecting the radiance of the One who has captivated our hearts. Let us love with His love, serve with His heart, and minister to Him first and foremost, trusting that as we pour ourselves out as drink offerings before Him, He will use us to ignite the nations with the fire of His holy passion.

The Bridegroom is coming, and He is looking for those who have made themselves ready---those whose hearts are fully His and whose lives are wholly abandoned to His purposes. May we be found among that company, clothed in garments of pure and spotless devotion, with lamps filled to overflowing with the oil of our extravagant love for Him.

Come, Lord Jesus, come! Have Your way in us and through us. Let Your Kingdom come and Your will be done on earth as it is in heaven. Amen and amen.

DEAR READER,

As you may have experienced for yourself, spending time with Christ is truly a life-changing and transformative experience. Whether you were moved to tears by the beauty of His words, to awe at the power of His presence, or simply filled with joy at the knowledge that you are loved and cherished by Him, we know that your life has been touched in some way by this book and we give Him all the glory!

We here at Refuge Ministries are so grateful for that. We believe wholeheartedly in the presence of God and the healing anointing it holds, and we are so grateful whenever our online community is brought together through our books, articles or our Refuge Ministries app found at our website. At Refuge, we strive every day to help people like you find refuge in God's presence. We are committed to spreading the love of Christ and living as intentionally as possible in his holy divine presence.

So, if this book has impacted you, please share your story on our website. www.findrefuge.tv Whether giving hope or strengthening faith, your testimony makes a difference. Thank you for participating in this bridal movement. As you go through your day, stay mindful of His manifest presence surrounding you. May your heart be warmed by His love and your spirit strengthened. Go in peace, resting in the Savior's constant love and guidance. We appreciate you reading and joining us on this journey! May you be ever mindful of the divine manifest presence that surrounds you. May your heart be warmed by His love and may your spirit be forever strengthened. Go forth in peace, knowing that you are always loved and guided by the beautiful Savior. Thank you for reading!

Consumed by His Presence,
Steve Porter
www.findrefuge.tv

The Manifest Presence of God: My Spiritual Journey
REVISED and ENLARGED EDITION By Walter Beuttler
is now available in English, Spanish, and German! Available
on Amazon, Kindle, www.findrefuge.tv
and wherever ebooks are sold!

30

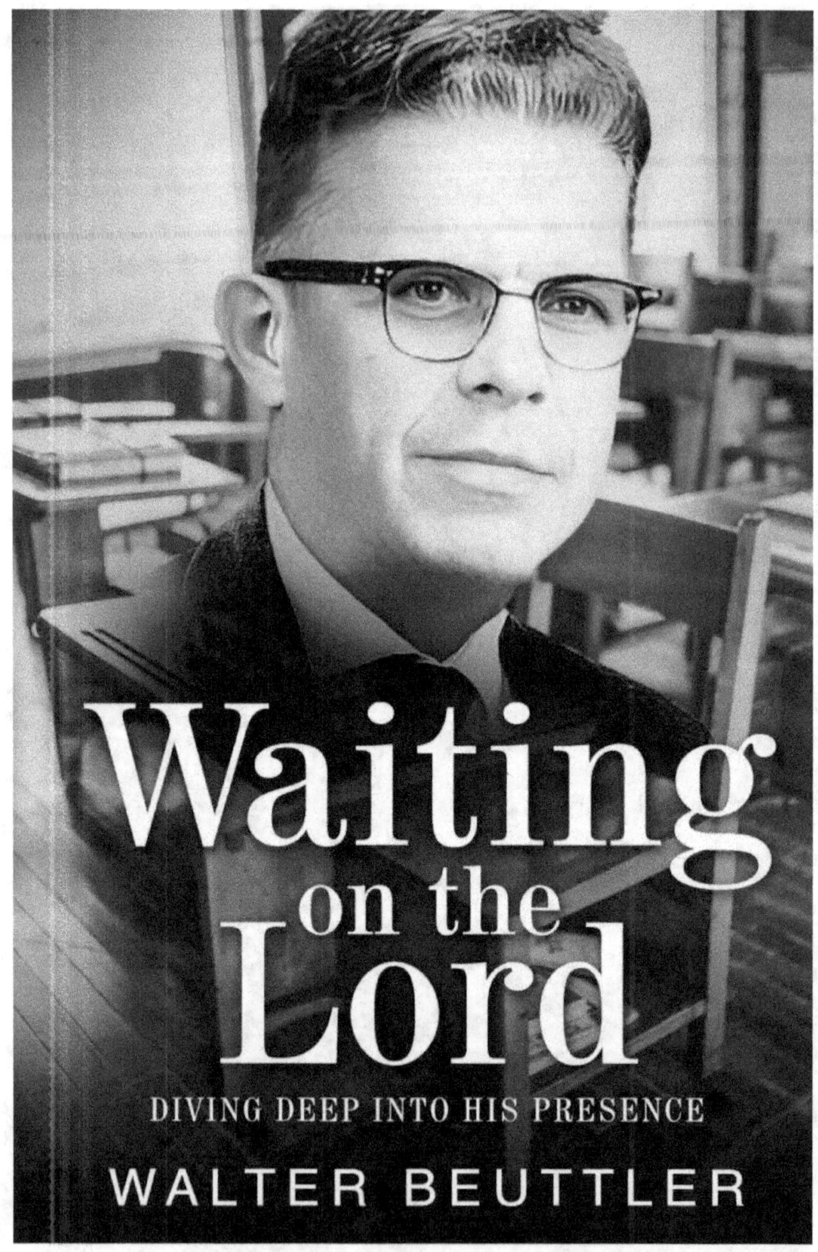
Waiting
on the
Lord
DIVING DEEP INTO HIS PRESENCE
WALTER BEUTTLER

<u>More Books by Steve & Diane Porter</u>

Garden of the Heart- *Healing Letters to Ladies* (Diane Porter)

Crocodile Meat- *New and Extended Version* (Steve's Life Story)

Crocodile Meat- *Student Version*

Whispers from the Throne Room- *Reflections on the Manifest Presence*

Limitless

He Leads Me Beside Still Waters- *50 Love Letters of Healing and Restoration from Our Lord*

Streams in the Desert- *Healing Letters for the Wounded Heart*

Invading the Darkness- *Power Evangelism Training 101*

Pearls of His Presence- *Intimate Devotions for the Spiritually Hungry*

The Tongue of the Learned- *How to Flow in the Prophetic Anointing*

Draw Me- *The Deep Cry of the Bride*

The Beauty of the Lord- *Your Keys to Radiating the Glory of God*

Hidden Treasure- *Intimate Devotions for the Spiritually Hungry*

Daniel Nash- *Laborer with Finney. Mighty in Prayer*

His Hands Extended- *Stories of Love at the Nursing Home* (Diane Porter)

Reflections for a Deeper Life

The Way of the Master- *A Teaching Tale and More*

Musing of a Watchman- A Compilation of Spiritual Writings- Volume 1

Musing of a Watchman- A Compilation of Spiritual Writings- Volume 2

Sowing in the Spirit- Investing into the Manifest Presence of God

Christ's Golden Queen- *A Prophetic View of Psalm 45*

The Great Holiness Revival Is Here!- *The Magnificent Beauty of His Holiness*

The Overcomers - A Compilation of Spiritual Writings for the Mature Sons and Mature Bride

<u>*Coming in 2024*</u>

<u>*by Steve & Diane Porter*</u>

Thirsty Waters- *Intimate Devotions for the Spiritually Hungry*

Into His Chambers- *Intimate Devotions for the Spiritually Hungry*

Drawing Near- *Intimate Devotions for the Spiritually Hungry*

Attracting The Presence of God- *7 Keys to A Special Touch from God*

*Bulk orders and international orders are available upon request. Email for details or order directly online.

Oasis Bible Training Center Spring Quarter 2024 and Grand Opening!

As you enter the Finger Lakes region of New York State, its stunning beauty capture your heart and fills it with awe. The sweet floral aromas that swirl around you join forces with the soothing whisper of rustling leaves to create a peaceful symphony in honor of God's greatness. Bathed in sunshine, this paradise is truly breathtaking!

But it's not just the natural beauty that draws you in. It's the palpable sense of His manifest presence that fills the air at Oasis Bible Training Center. As you walk through the halls of the training center, you feel a stirring in your soul, a yearning for something deeper, something more.

This school founded by Steve & Diane Porter believes in building God a house of devotion and then knowing God will build a house of ministry. The community at Oasis is unlike any other, a tight-knit group of individuals all seeking to deepen their connection with the Spirit. The warmth of their smiles and the kindness of their words make you feel instantly at home, and you realize that this is a place where you can truly grow in your spiritual journey.

With our grand opening and the launch of the Spring Quarter quickly approaching, the anticipation is electric. Attendees from all over are eager to experience the transformative power of God's love and guidance. The training center is a place where you can spread your wings and soar, discovering new depths of yourself and the Spirit.

Come and join us at Oasis Bible Training Center, where your soul will awaken to the beauty of His manifest presence. Let your heart be filled with passion and fire as you journey towards a deeper intimacy with the sweet Master Jesus. Here, you'll find a community of like-minded individuals, all seeking to build a house of devotion unto the Lord. So why wait? Come and discover the wonders that await you at Oasis!

Oasis operates as a faith-based school, providing education without charging any enrollment fees. We warmly welcome anyone who wishes to become a student, regardless of their financial situation. Our reliance is placed entirely on faith, trusting that God will provide for all our financial needs and support the continued operation of our school. For more information and registration. www.oasisbible.org

The Deeper Life is our premiere quarterly publication designed to inspire spiritual growth and transformation in people's lives. This publication is a rare treasure for those who are desperately hungry during these end times. It is a special bridal tool designed to bring forth spiritual growth. *The Deeper Life* publication is a must-read for those longing for more of the Heavenly Bridegroom. Be on the lookout for our newest edition of **The Deeper Life** each season—Spring, Summer, Fall, and Winter! We hope you will collect them all! Available worldwide or at www.oasisbible.org

(Pamphlets for those that want to go deeper spiritually)

Spiritual Maturity Tracts by Steve Porter now available!

See our website

www.findrefuge.tv

R

Refuge Ministries

182 Lincoln Rd

Newark, NY 14513

www.findrefuge.tv

www.deeperlifepress.com